A Guide to the Deities of the Tantra

A Guide to the Deities of the Tantra

Vessantara

Windhorse Publications

Originally published as Part 4 of *Meeting the Buddhas* 1993
Revised and published as *A Guide to the Deities of the Tantra* 2008

Published by Windhorse Publications Ltd
38 Newmarket Road
Cambridge
CB5 8DT
UK

Cover design Sagarapriya

Printed by The Cromwell Press Ltd, Trowbridge, England

Cover image: Padmasambhava painting by Aloka
reproduced by permission of Padmaloka Retreat Centre

British Library Cataloguing in Publication Data
A catalogue record for this book is available from the British Library

ISBN 978 1 899579 85 3

Contents

	About the Author	vii
One	The Tantric Approach	1
Two	Prajñāpāramitā – the Book that Became a Goddess	19
Three	Vajrasattva – Prince of Purity	31
Four	The Esoteric Buddha and the Lotus-Born Guru	47
Five	The Oath-Bound Deities	71
Six	Dancing in the Sky	93
Seven	The Dark Armies of the Dharma	111
Eight	The Refuge Tree and its Future Growth	141
	Notes	149
	Illustration Credits	157
	Glossary	159
	Selected Reading	169
	Index	173

Illustrations

Colour

Plate One	Heruka Cakrasaṃvara
Plate Two	Vajrabhairava
Plate Three	Kālacakra
Plate Four	Vajravārāhī
Plate Five	Vajrayoginī as Sarvabuddhaḍākinī
Plate Six	Mahākāla
Plate Seven	Śrīdevī
Plate Eight	Refuge Assembly

Monochrome

Page 14	Śrī Mahā Heruka
Page 18	Prajñāpāramitā
Page 30	Vajrasattva
Page 34	Heruka Vajrasattva
Page 46	Padmasambhava
Page 52	Padmasambhava as Urgyen Dorje Chang
Page 62	Milarepa
Page 70	Vajrabhairava
Page 92	Chöd ḍākinī
Page 100	Machik Labdron
Page 102	Siṃhamukha
Page 110	The Four Great Kings
Page 118	Mahākāla
Page 120	Śrīdevī
Page 132	Refuge Assembly
Page 136	Samantabhadra and Samantabhadri
Page 138	Vajradhara

About the Author

Vessantara is a senior member of the Western Buddhist Order. Born Tony McMahon in London in 1950, he gained an MA in English at Cambridge University. He became interested in Buddhism in his teens, and first had direct contact with Buddhists in 1971. In 1974 he was ordained and given the name Vessantara, which means 'universe within'.

In 1975 he gave up a career in social work to become more involved with the development of the Friends of the Western Buddhist Order. Since then he has divided his time between meditating, studying, and assisting the development of several Buddhist centres, including retreat centres in England, Wales, and Spain.

Vessantara is much in demand as a Buddhist teacher. For seven years he led three-month courses for people entering the Order and now gives talks and leads retreats and workshops throughout Europe and Australasia.

He has written written several books, including *Tales of Freedom, The Mandala of the Five Buddhas, The Vajra and Bell*, and *Female Deities in Buddhism*.

One

The Tantric Approach

A peaceful and saintly Tibetan monk sits in his monastery. His room is virtually dark. It is hard to discern anything. As our eyes become accustomed to the dim light they take in a scene that is at odds with the serene expression of the monk. In lurid, gory detail, monstrous shapes brandishing terrifying weapons stare menacingly from the dark paintings on the walls. Hung from the ceiling are the carcasses of wild beasts. In the jumbled Sanskrit of the mantras the lama is reciting we make out the words 'Kill! Kill! Trample, destroy!'

A young woman carries her purchases through a new shopping mall. She sees the giant store as a beautiful mandala palace. The checkout girls and shoppers are gods and goddesses. She imagines that the background music is the mantra of her chosen deity. She treats her desire for a chocolate bar as though it were the wisdom of a Buddha.

A wild-eyed man stands in a cremation ground. He is dressed with ornaments made of human bone. He produces a musical instrument from the folds of his clothing. It is a human thighbone. He stares about him. In his imagination he is conducting his own funeral. His corpse has been transmuted into an ocean of nectar, upon which sentient beings are invited to feast.

A celibate nun imagines herself locked in sexual union with a young lover. During the embrace she offers him a cup fashioned from a human skull, and pours the red liquid it contains into his mouth. She tells her spiritual teacher that this fantasy is taking on a tremendous reality for her. The guru is pleased with her progress.

I have chosen these examples as stark demonstrations of the very different world we are entering in this book. The two previous books in this series, *A Guide to the Buddhas* and *A Guide to the Bodhisattvas*, introduced readers to the various Buddhas and Bodhisattvas described in the Buddhist sutras. They are thus part of the world of the Mahāyāna. Their descriptions are illuminated by a Mahāyāna world-view. Most of them are calm and serene, exuding the great love (Sanskrit *mahāmaitrī*) and great compassion (Sanskrit *mahākaruṇā*) which conjoined with transcendental wisdom constitute the perfect expression of Enlightenment in the Mahāyāna sūtras. The one glaring exception (literally) was the wrathful form of Vajrapāṇi. He was an omen of what is to come in this final book of the series.

The Hīnayāna and Mahāyāna schools are collectively designated the Sūtrayāna, because they are based on the sūtras. The sūtras are carefully preserved records of the Buddha's oral teachings, or the teachings of advanced disciples that were approved by the Buddha. The Pali suttas of the Hīnayāna give factual accounts of the Buddha's life and teaching. We see him seated in jungle clearings or calmly walking the dusty Indian roads. Everywhere he goes, he teaches. His teaching is pragmatic, avoiding all metaphysical speculation. In essence it is all related to suffering, and the practical methods for overcoming it. There are miraculous events, such as the 'twin miracle', where the Buddha is represented rising into the air and producing fire and water from his body simultaneously. Most of the time, though, we are in the everyday world, being taught how to work patiently with our mental states to overcome craving, hatred, and ignorance. That done, we can see life as it really is, and attain the deathless state.

Reading the Mahāyāna sūtras we find ourselves on the very summit of existence. The Buddha sits on a Vulture's Peak[1] that no Indian traveller would recognize. He is Śākyamuni transfigured, emanating light from his body to call Buddhas to visit him from distant universes. Dimensions expand and contract. Miraculous beings appear from nowhere in the midst of the vast assembly of Bodhisattvas and arhats who are listening to the Buddha's discourse. The medium of these sūtras is the message. An infinite number of universes are embraced by the Buddha's compassion, just as his radiance lights up endless galaxies. The teaching is subtle, mysterious, ungraspable. The intellect is confounded by Perfect Wisdom, which defies the laws of logic, just as the Buddha's display of psychic powers transcends the laws of science. Our hearts expand to embrace all beings, just as the Bodhisattva appears everywhere, in all realms, in his tireless work of salvation. The Mahāyāna sūtras appeal to the imagination. Their cosmic drama lifts us out of our mundane world and everyday selves into the archetypal realm. We are shown a vision of the Ultimate, beyond duality, beyond time and space.

Any approach to human development can become one-sided or stagnant. After a while, the Hīnayāna approach tended to fall into dogmatic literalism, and to spend much time in academic classification of negative and positive psychological states, rather than getting down to the job of transforming one into the other. The Mahāyāna's rich imagination overcame any tendency to dogmatism and narrowness. Its radical reduction of all concepts to śūnyatā put the academic categories of the Hīnayāna in their proper perspective. However, the Mahāyāna also fell prey at times to certain dangers. Rejoicing in the subtle sharpness of its dialectic, entranced by its archetypal glory, the feet of some Mahāyāna followers began to lose touch with the ground of everyday reality.

The attempt to counterbalance this tendency of the Mahāyāna finds expression in the Vajrayāna ('way of the diamond thunderbolt'). The Vajrayāna is synonymous with the Buddhist Tantric schools. The Hīnayāna, at its worst, had kept its feet on the ground of direct experience, but lost touch with its spiritual imagination. The Mahāyāna occasionally lost its head in the golden clouds of the archetypal. The Vajrayāna, in a radical stroke of genius, aimed to see the archetypal in the everyday, the exalted goal of nirvāṇa in the mud and dust of saṃsāra. It fused Hīnayāna pragmatism and Mahāyāna imagination into the vajra of the Tantric approach to life. (I am not suggesting that these waves of counterbalancing reactions between schools were conscious. They were probably largely intuitive.) By and large, the followers of Tantra did not deny the Mahāyāna approach. They saw it simply as a foundation on which to lay down their unique approach to Enlightenment.

The Vajrayāna teachings find their authority not in the sūtras but in the Buddhist tantras. *Sūtra* literally means thread. Each sūtra contains a teaching by the Buddha that has a logical thread or continuity to it. *Tantra*, however, means something woven. This suggests an added dimension. The tantras are not usually logically connected pieces of teaching. It is as though the threads of the sūtras have been woven into a tapestry, in which the continuity of any individual thread may be lost from sight.

The tantras are all attributed to Śākyamuni – usually under his Tantric name of Buddha Vajradhara – and it is claimed that their teachings were bestowed by him in secret. When you attempt to relate to the everyday through the archetypal, or to manipulate spiritual forces through natural ones, what you are involved in is magic. The contents of the tantras are a witch's brew of magical spells and rituals, yogic instructions and profound teachings, often in jumbled fragments which make them unintelligible to the uninitiated. They are like the grimoires of an Enlightened wizard – who practises a transcendental magic that cannot be said to be either black or white.

The fact that Tantric texts often make little sense to a reader unprovided with the keys for deciphering them underlines the central importance of the guru in the Tantra. As we shall see in Chapter Four, the guru occupies the centre of the mandala of Tantric practice. It is through him that realization dawns. In fact, traditionally one cannot even step onto the Tantric path without the guru, for it is he who opens the gates to each stage of the path by bestowing initiation.

Tantric practices and their associated initiations are divided into different levels. Most Tibetan schools recognize four main ones: *kriyā* (action), *caryā* (performance), *yoga* (union), and *anuttarayoga* (supreme union).[2] The first three are known collectively as the Lower Tantras; their practice involves more external rituals.

The *anuttarayoga*, or Highest Tantra, needs no external ritual at all. At each level of Tantra one is introduced to a different degree of understanding, and one's relationship to the Buddha, Bodhisattva, or other Tantric deity around which the ritual centres changes. The higher the tantra, the more intimate the relationship – the more totally identified you become with the state of Buddhahood. Highest Tantra is itself divided by most Tibetan schools into the two stages of *kyerim*, the generation stage, and *dzokrim*, the completion stage. In the generation stage you work to identify yourself as completely as possible with an aspect of Enlightenment through visualization. This serves as preparation for the completion stage, which is concerned with the manipulation of subtle psychophysical energies in order to bring about a profound transformation of consciousness.

However, rather than become involved in a lengthy analysis of the technicalities of the Tantric tradition, we shall concentrate on the underlying principles of Tantra. If we can set these cornerstones in place we shall understand the essentials. Then we shall be able to approach the Tantra with confidence, without being bewildered by the extraordinary luxuriance of its forms. To do this, we are going to look in turn at seven characteristics of the Vajrayāna.

1 Tantra is concerned with direct experience

We saw that Tantra developed partly in response to the Mahāyāna tendency to lose touch with the everyday world. Tantra is pragmatic. It has a critical 'how does it actually help?' approach to spiritual teachings. However fine your ideas, however beautiful your imaginative fantasies, if some aspect of Buddhism makes no difference to your actual experience, the Tantra is not interested. It tries to make everything directly accessible and usable. If you have not had a particular spiritual experience, it asks you to find whatever in your personal experience corresponds with it.

For example, it is as though the Tantra says, 'You say you take Refuge in the Buddha. But Śākyamuni Buddha died 2,500 years ago. If you were very highly spiritually developed you might still feel his spiritual influence, but what if you're not? You need direct contact to inspire you, not just books. So if you've missed out on Śākyamuni, who in your own experience comes closest to being Enlightened? Who are you in actual contact with who is most like a Buddha?... Your guru? All right then, as far as you are concerned your guru is the Buddha, your Buddha Refuge.' The Tantra does the same with the other refuges, as we shall see in Chapters Five and Six.

Tantra, then, aims to enable you to experience the truths of Buddhism directly. It is not interested in theories and ideas *per se*. Like Zen, it asks to be shown, here and now in this room, non-duality, śūnyatā, compassion, and all those other fine-sounding ideas. A Buddhist teacher once produced an aphorism 'work is the Tantric guru'. If you are building a wall, it is either there at the end of the day or it is not. Your ideas about what lovely walls you could build count for nothing. Hard work gives you objective feedback on your capacity to mobilize your energy and get things done. It demands a great deal of you. You really have to give yourself to it. All these things are true also of the Tantric guru, and the Tantric approach. It demands hard work and dedication to actualize the Tantric path.

Tantra is often said to be a quick path to Enlightenment. People become excited by this, but in the spiritual life you never obtain something for nothing. Unless your karma is exceptionally good, before you can truly enter upon the Vajrayāna you need long preparation in the Sūtrayāna. In addition, the practice of Tantra requires great effort, energy, and determination. As another aphorism says, 'The Tantra is quick and easy, if you work long enough and hard enough!'

2 Tantra works with symbols and magic

If the Tantra is to be a quick path, it has to effect a radical transformation of your whole being, both conscious and unconscious. The Sūtrayāna addresses itself to both head and heart, but not so directly to the unconscious. If you want to involve that level of yourself in the quest for Enlightenment, you have to communicate with it and win over its energies. What language can you use to do so?

We could compare the human psyche to a great city like London or Rome. On the surface it is full of the life and concerns of the twenty-first century, but those banks and office blocks have been erected over the rubble of previous buildings. We can dig down through various strata to earlier periods. Now we find a Roman villa, now a pagan temple, now a primitive earthwork fortification. Something similar can be seen in the development of the human psyche. We live our lives as more or less self-conscious, rational beings. Yet the level of consciousness we have reached is the latest stage of a process going back over millennia.

As far as we can tell, primitive man had little self-consciousness. He lived in a twilight, dream-like world, unable fully to differentiate between his inner and outer reality. It is as though, in the unconscious, we carry this racial memory. Our consciousness, too, has 'strata' – some of which are not rational at all. We become aware of them in dreams, and in other situations where archetypal contents well up into the light of consciousness.

To communicate with these deeper strata we have to speak their language. That language is the language of myth, symbol, and magic. Magic is the 'technology' that primitive man used to control his world. To transform our primitive depths we cannot give them lectures on impermanence and śūnyatā, we have to resort to magic.

The Tantra, then, borrowed magical rites from its ethnic context and turned them to its own purposes. We can see this in sādhanas connected with the five Buddha families of the mandala (see Glossary). Akṣobhya is associated with the poison of hatred, which he transmutes into wisdom. The Tantra does this by taking magical rituals of destruction and changing their aim. Instead of destroying rivals and enemies, the rites have been refined so that they now eradicate hatred and hindrances to gaining Enlightenment.

Ratnasambhava, the yellow Buddha associated with the earth, is connected with harvest magic – in fact with all rites of increase. The Tantric magician uses this magic to increase his or her energy, compassion, understanding of the Dharma, and so on.

Amitābha, the red Buddha of love, is naturally the patron of rites of fascination. Rather than practise these to compel a lover to return, the yogin or yogini causes all beings to fall in love with the Dharma.

Vairocana – serene in the centre of the mandala – holds sway over rites of pacification.[3] Again, it is the waves of negative emotion that his rites pacify. Amoghasiddhi's all-performing wisdom allows him to be associated with success in all forms of magic, to gain the supreme *siddhi*, or magic power, of gaining Enlightenment.

The Tantric adept is even referred to as a *siddha* – one who has attained magic powers. These powers can be supernormal (such as levitation, telepathy, etc.) or involve the development of spiritual qualities. There is a well-known group of eighty-four (sometimes eighty-five) *mahāsiddhas* (great Tantric adepts), who flourished in India from the eighth to twelfth centuries. They form the beginning of a chain of human Tantric practitioners who have carried on the major forms of Tantric practice to this day. The lives of these eighty-four Indian men and women abound in episodes that demonstrate the magical power over natural phenomena that they have gained through Tantric practice.

3 Tantra addresses the whole person

As we have seen, Tantra is pragmatic and down to earth. It will not leave any aspect of us untransformed. Buddhism distinguishes three aspects to a human being – body, speech, and mind, and a Tantric practice will usually involve all of them. The body may be involved through making prostrations, turning prayer wheels, circumambulating, making physical offerings, or mudrā. We have seen how Buddhas and Bodhisattvas are depicted making mudrās that express their spiritual qualities. The Tantric practitioner also employs mudrā, using the body as a support for meditation by thus involving it. For the Vajrayāna, a spiritual experience is not complete until it has percolated right through to your fingertips.

Speech is involved through recitation, especially of mantras. The mind is given complex symbolic visualizations to dwell on. In this way the Vajrayāna weaves patterns of practice that involve your total being.

4 Tantra sees the world in terms of energy

If you practise the Dharma in an orderly fashion, you only take up the practice of the Vajrayāna once you have deep experience of the Mahāyāna. *Mahā* means great (so the Mahāyāna is the 'great way' to Enlightenment). However, *mahā* also often implies 'conjoined with śūnyatā' (see Glossary). For instance *mahākaruṇā*, the 'great compassion' of the Bodhisattva, is the compassion that has arisen out of the experience of śūnyatā.

So if you follow the path of regular steps, as it is called, you only embark on Tantra once you have passed through the flames of śūnyatā in Mahāyāna practice.

If you have passed through those flames, and transmuted your consciousness within them, how do you see the world? If the substantial objects and people, the discrete, separate selfhoods, have all been dissolved into processes, ever changing, then what is left? What you experience are patterns of energy, some more congealed, others more free-flowing. Tantric practice, then, is very much concerned with energy.

In particular, Tantra works with very subtle levels of energy within the human body. In some advanced Tantric practices you visualize a whole subtle energy system, composed of channels, winds, and drops (Sanskrit *nāḍī, prāṇa*, and *bindu*).[4] Through directing the subtle energy flow through visualization, the energies are led into the central channel (Sanskrit *avadhūtī*, Tibetan *tsa uma*), located in front of the spine. (Here, though, we are working on the level of the subtle, visualized body; relating it to the spine enables us to visualize it in the right location, it does not imply that the central channel is on the same plane of reality as the physical spine.) Once the subtle energies, or winds, have entered one or another of the cakras, the subtle energy centres of the central channel, a particularly deep level of concentration is attained. Through meditation on śūnyatā while in this state, the Tantra claims you can gain Enlightenment very quickly. It is the use of meditation on this subtle energy system, not found in the other yānas, which it is claimed can make the Vajrayāna a 'short path' to Enlightenment.

In this state of deep concentration, when the winds dissolve in the central channel, one experiences the mental phenomena that happen at the time of death. If the Tantric yogin or yogini has already experienced these phenomena in meditation, it enables them to go through the actual death experience, when the time comes, with awareness and control. In this way they can either transcend the endless round of birth and death altogether, or select a place and form of rebirth in which they can be most helpful to other beings.

5 Tantra makes use of the strongest experiences of life

Because the Vajrayāna experiences the universe as a play of energy, it has no reason to reject any experience. All expressions of energy, even seemingly negative ones, are grist to its mill. If you see things in terms of fixed entities, then you have to reject certain experiences. If you see the world as energy, then at worst you will see energy temporarily locked into limiting or negative patterns. However, you will also see that energy as a resource, a potential which can be liberated. For the car owner, a wrecked car is useless, something to be towed away. For the scrap dealer it is a resource. Its raw materials can be melted down to make brand new cars.

For this reason, the Vajrayāna works with negative emotions in different ways from the Sūtrayāna. The Hīnayāna approach is to use mindfulness to hold feelings of craving and hatred at arm's length. The Vajrayāna, however, accepts these feelings as expressions of Reality just like any other, and as powerful energies to be transmuted. It is because the Tantra rejoices in these energies that it has often been misunderstood. Some people have criticized it as a mere licence to indulge, others have *used* it as a mere licence to indulge! We can see here why Tantric training has to be built on experience of the other two yānas. The Tantric practitioner has to have enough insight and self-discipline to play with fire – to ride the most raw and powerful energies of the human psyche on the road to liberation. Without sufficient prior training they will soon throw you and drag you along in an entirely different direction....

We can now begin to understand what the monk, the nun, and the yogin were doing at the beginning of our chapter. The Vajrayāna looks at life to see where the most potent energies are to be found, then works to harness them. It does not have to search far. It finds craving and aversion exerting their spells most strongly in the areas of sex and death. So it uses imagery connected with these two great pillars of saṃsāra (as we might call them) to transmute the tremendous powers locked within them.

Visualizing beautiful and handsome forms made of light can have a refining, sublimating effect on our erotic drives. However, the Tantra goes further than gazing at, or even becoming, an attractive young Bodhisattva made of light. It uses sexually explicit imagery. It shows Buddhas locked in union with beautiful consorts, in a variety of poses. These *yab-yum* (a Tibetan phrase meaning father-mother)[5] couples are regarded with particular reverence by Vajrayāna devotees, as expressions of the highest truth.

To take an example, in the Vajrayāna the five Buddhas are frequently shown seated in a sexual embrace with female consorts. In this case we have to understand that the *yab-yum* couple is really one figure. Just as the four Buddhas around Vairocana are all facets of his Dharmadhātu Wisdom, so when a Buddha takes a *yab-yum* form this is a way of making explicit different aspects of the Enlightened experience which that Buddha represents. In a *yab-yum* figure, the female represents the wisdom aspect of the Enlightened experience, so she is often referred to as the *prajñā*, or wisdom, of the Buddha. The male symbolizes the method or skilful means through which that wisdom is compassionately expressed in the world.

Let us briefly meet the consorts of the five Buddhas of the mandala. Entering this mandala from the east, we see Akṣobhya embracing his blue consort Locanā. Locanā means 'she with the eye'. She expresses the clear seeing of the mirror-like wisdom.

In the south, Ratnasambhava embraces the yellow Māmakī. Māmakī means 'mine maker' – not in the sense of mines of jewels, though. Māmakī feels for all living beings as though they were her own children, her own self. They are all hers. She feels as though the whole universe is hers. When you possess her wisdom you think of everything as 'mine'. When everything is yours, when you feel for everyone, then is born the wisdom of equality.

In the west, Amitābha embraces the red Pāṇḍaravāsinī (white-robed one). Pāṇḍaravāsinī is sometimes said to be a form of White Tārā. Her white robe also suggests the simile given by the Buddha for the feeling of someone experiencing the fourth dhyāna, or meditative absorption. In this state, the Buddha says, you are like someone who on a very hot day takes a cool bath, and then puts on a fresh white robe. White reflects the sun, and radiates light. Similarly, in the fourth dhyāna your mind is so positive that its influence radiates and can even positively affect your environment and other people. So Pāṇḍaravāsinī perhaps expresses not only the discriminating wisdom, but also aspects of meditative experience – with which Amitābha is especially linked through his dhyāna mudrā.

In the north, Amoghasiddhi's consort is Green Tārā. Her fearless compassion and instant response to the needs of living beings are expressions of the All-Accomplishing Wisdom.

Finally, coming to the centre of the mandala, in its white radiance we see Vairocana in union with the white Ākāśadhāteśvarī ('sovereign lady of the sphere of infinite space'). Here, the complementary nature of *yab* and *yum* is clearly shown. Vairocana ('illuminator') radiates the light of Buddhahood. Yet for light to radiate there must be space for it to pass through. In the Dharmadhātu Wisdom, light and Emptiness dance together, and are united in one experience.

We shall meet with much more sexual imagery in the coming chapters. If we can use such visualizations without being pulled into straightforward sexual desire, then some of the most powerful energies of our psyche will be invested in the quest for Enlightenment.

The Vajrayāna also employs imagery connected with death. It loves to use ritual implements made of human bone: there are bone rosaries for counting mantras, trumpets made from human femurs, cups made from human skulls. It employs these things as reminders of death, to accustom us to impermanence. As death is usually what is most feared, handling the remnants of death develops, and symbolizes, fearlessness. Bone implements and skulls are also emblems of śūnyatā, because with the experience of śūnyatā one's concept of oneself as a fixed ego-entity disappears. Viewed from the standpoint of someone who has not experienced insight into Reality, and still conceives of themself as a fixed ego, the experience of śūnyatā can only appear to be a kind of death.

Weapons and violence are associated with death. In the coming chapters we shall meet powerfully built figures with ferocious expressions brandishing axes, choppers, lassoes, and other medieval battle implements.

The Vajrayāna uses magic ritual, and the magical traditions of both East and West have made much symbolic use of weapons for attack or defence against hostile forces. The Tantra uses swords, thunderbolts, and so on, and visualization of wrathful figures, to sublimate aggression and violent tendencies and to express the power of wisdom to smash illusion and hack down suffering.

To give some idea what these wrathful figures are like, we shall take as examples the five Buddhas of the mandala. The *Tibetan Book of the Dead* describes the appearance, in the bardo or after-death state, of their peaceful forms. These are all expressions of Reality, but if one fails to perceive their empty nature and becomes frightened by them, then from a more alienated perspective Reality begins to assume threatening forms. On the eighth day in the bardo, the Glorious Great Buddha Heruka appears. He is a wrathful deity, powerfully built, and wreathed in flames. His body is the colour of wine. He has six arms, three heads, and four legs. The text describes him in graphic detail:

> His body blazes like a mass of light, his nine eyes gaze into yours with a wrathful expression, his eyebrows are like flashes of lightning, his teeth gleam like copper; he laughs aloud with shouts of 'a-la-la!' and 'ha-ha!' and sends out loud whistling noises of 'shoo-oo!'.[6]

He stands on a throne supported by garuḍas. He is locked in sexual embrace with his consort Buddha Krodheśvarī. Though he appears extremely threatening, the text urges you to recognize him as the wrathful form of the white Buddha Vairocana.

Over the four succeeding days, four more Herukas – Buddhas in wrathful form – appear with their consorts. Each is the wrathful form of one of the peaceful Buddhas: Akṣobhya, Ratnasambhava, Amitābha, Amoghasiddhi, and Vairocana. Their names show their association with the five Buddha families: Vajra Heruka, Ratna Heruka, Padma Heruka, Karma Heruka, and Buddha Heruka. Their bodies are of a colour corresponding to that of their peaceful form, but rather darker. So, for example, the Karma Heruka, who appears on the twelfth day, is green like Amoghasiddhi, but of a darker shade.

Śrī Mahā Heruka

An overview of this book

Armed with these short explanations of some features of Tantra, we can now encounter the Tantric deities. In Chapter Two, we meet Prajñāpāramitā, who acts as a kind of bridge. She is the only figure in this book who also appears in the sūtras. As we shall see, she personifies a set of sūtras, transmuted into a goddess through the Tantric desire for direct experience. Then comes Vajrasattva, the 'diamond being', invoked for purification by followers of the 'diamond way'. In Chapters Four to Six we meet the esoteric, Tantric forms of the Three Jewels. Buddha, Dharma, and Sangha are experienced through gurus, yidams, and ḍākinīs. In the following chapter, if we are feeling strong, we can encounter the *dharmapālas*, the Tantric protectors of the Dharma. Finally, in Chapter Eight, we put together the jigsaw puzzle of figures we have met into the great uniting symbol of the Refuge Tree.

Prajñāpāramitā

Two

Prajñāpāramitā – the Book that Became a Goddess

One October night in 1816, Charles Cowden Clarke sat up late in his rooms in London, reading and talking with a young friend. Clarke and his friend loved literature, and they had managed to lay hands on a copy of Homer, translated by Chapman. It was dawn by the time they stopped reading and discussing. After his friend had gone, Clarke took a few hours sleep. On coming down to breakfast he found a note waiting for him. It was a perfectly turned sonnet from his fellow reader:

> Much have I travelled in the realms of gold,
> And many goodly states and kingdoms seen;
> Round many western islands have I been
> Which bards in fealty to Apollo hold.
> Oft of one wide expanse had I been told
> That deep-browed Homer ruled as his demesne:
> Yet did I never breathe its pure serene
> Till I heard Chapman speak out loud and bold:
> Then felt I like some watcher of the skies
> When a new planet swims into his ken;
> Or like stout Cortez when with eagle eyes
> He stared at the Pacific – and all his men
> Looked at each other with a wild surmise –
> Silent, upon a peak in Darien.[7]

Clarke's friend can only have had two or three hours in which to produce his poem. It would be an achievement for any poet to fashion something so fine so quickly, and after a sleepless night. For a twenty-year-old it was extraordinary. That breakfast-time note to Clarke was one of the first declarations of the poetic genius of his friend John Keats.

The 'realms of gold' in which Keats has travelled are of course the worlds of literature, of the imagination. (Among other things, Apollo is the god of poetry.) Through his poem we can remind ourselves of the tremendous value and power not just of literature, but of the written word.

Nowadays we are glutted with print. So surfeited are we that it is easy to take books for granted. We can buy the thoughts of the world's greatest minds, and read them on the bus. However, the mass production of literature is still quite a new development. Six or seven centuries ago every book was precious, for they all had to be painstakingly hand-copied. A prince with a hundred volumes would have possessed a large library.

If you were a scholar at that time you would have had to wander from place to place – from one library to the next. You might have heard of a book and had to travel hundreds of miles to consult one of the few copies in existence. If you had wanted to study it intensively you would have had to stay where the book was kept, or copied it yourself, which might have taken months – even if you did not embellish the book, as was often done in the scriptoria of the monasteries. Or you might have travelled with your library on your back – like Marpa returning home to Tibet with the teachings he had gathered in India. And, like Marpa, you might easily have lost those hard-gained volumes.[8]

How would we feel if we had copied by hand all the books in our possession? How much more would we value them? Even for Keats, much closer to our own time, a new book was a treasure.

We need somehow to regain this feeling of appreciation, even of reverence, for books, if we are to begin to enter into a proper relationship with the Perfection of Wisdom literature. If even ordinary books can be so precious, then books containing the highest insights of humanity must be extraordinary treasures indeed.

Ordinary books are valuable because they crystallize and preserve knowledge, memories, ideas, and experience. The Perfection of Wisdom literature encapsulates – as far as it is possible in words – the experience of Enlightenment. I am stressing this point because in almost any city in the Western world it is quite easy to buy a book of the Perfection of Wisdom and read that on the bus. How you read the Perfection of Wisdom (Sanskrit *Prajñāpāramitā*) literature is supremely important. One of the earliest Wisdom texts admonishes us in its opening line:

> Call forth as much as you can of love, of respect and of faith![9]

Gaining wisdom is at least as much a matter of becoming receptive emotionally as of intellectual acuity. This, as we shall see later, was one of the main reasons why the Perfection of Wisdom literature transformed itself into a goddess – to teach more effectively by appearing in a form that people would love to dwell upon.

For Keats, Chapman's Homer is a catalyst. While reading, his imagination starts to fly. He feels as though he has seen a new planet, or discovered a new ocean. Hernán Cortéz was the 'conquistador' who subdued the Aztecs. In the sonnet, though, he is a positive figure. Cortéz has landed on the Caribbean coast of modern-day Panama. He has walked inland with his men and climbed a peak, to discover an ocean vaster than the one he has just crossed, stretching away below him. Gazing at this new realm of possibility, he and his men are struck silent.[10]

Keats feels he has found a new vantage point in himself, seen possibilities he never knew existed. This should be the case when we first encounter the Perfection of Wisdom literature. The books themselves are just catalysts for a new vision of the universe. An undreamed of realm begins to unfold itself. If you enter fully into this golden realm, then, like Cortéz's men, words will fail you. You will be unable to describe what you have apprehended. Someone who has used the Prajñāpāramitā literature to enter the transcendental realm is said to be like a mute who has had a dream.

The development of the Perfection of Wisdom literature

According to tradition, the Perfection of Wisdom literature springs from Śākyamuni Buddha, but he found that the teachings were not appropriate for the men and women of his time, and shortly before his *parinirvāṇa*, or passing away, he entrusted the teachings to the nāgas.

Nāgas in Buddhist tradition have something of the same characteristics as dragons. They are long-lived, wise, and can function as guardians of treasures. Nāgas live at the bottom of the ocean, and it was in their watery kingdom that the Wisdom teachings were preserved. Several centuries later one of the greatest figures in Buddhist history, Nāgārjuna, came to the edge of a certain lake and received the Perfect Wisdom teachings from a nāga princess.

The first Perfection of Wisdom teachings appeared about 100 BCE. During a two hundred year phase of development the basic texts of the literature appeared. The oldest are probably the *Aṣṭasāhasrikā*, or *Perfection of Wisdom in 8,000 Lines*, and its verse counterpart, the *Ratnaguṇasaṃcayagāthā* (verses on the storehouse of precious virtues).

In the following 200 years the Perfection of Wisdom literature achieved great popularity. So much devotion was lavished upon it that it expanded. One text even reached 100,000 lines in length.

The succeeding 200 years (roughly 300–500 CE) saw the Perfection of Wisdom spread throughout India and into China. In this phase the new texts became increasingly concise. Among them are two of the most famous and important of all Buddhist works: the *Diamond Sūtra* (Sanskrit *Vajracchedikā*) and the *Heart Sūtra* (Sanskrit *Hṛdaya*).[11]

By the year 700, the process of contraction had gone as far as possible. There is a 'Perfection of Wisdom in a Few Words' which says it is for the 'dull and stupid'. There is even the 'Perfection of Wisdom in a Single Letter'! This is the letter A, which in Sanskrit is a negative prefix. It is as though the text says that whatever you think, however you try to describe the world, you should put the word 'not' before it. However you explain the universe, Reality is not that. The Perfection of Wisdom denies that you will ever catch Reality in the clumsy net of words and concepts, and breaks up your preconceptions about everything. You say you are of a certain age, sex, nationality, occupation, and so on. The 'Perfection of Wisdom in One Letter' denies that in Reality you are any of these things.

They are just the fool's gold of conventional descriptions, not the true gold of Reality.

Also during this period, something very remarkable happened. The Perfection of Wisdom, under the influence of the Tantra, began to change. This literature of uncompromising paradox and intellectual subtlety transformed itself. From being an intellectual thunderbolt, destroying conceptualizations, it was reborn as a wisdom goddess and a mantra. Examining this extraordinary 'sea change' can give us insights into the Tantric approach to self-transformation.

Tantra, we have seen, is always concerned with direct experience. Rather than denying words and concepts in the hope that you will reach beyond them, it employs a different approach. It tries to help you leave behind conceptualization by entering an imaginative realm. You enter a realm of light, travel in a realm of gold. In this archetypal realm you are brought face to face with Wisdom, in the most appealing form imaginable.

At about the time of Charlemagne, the figure of Prajñāpāramitā (Tibetan *Sherapkyi Pharoltuchinma*) as a Wisdom goddess began to appear in the East. She had different forms: sometimes golden, sometimes white. She appeared with two, four, or six arms, or even (in a form popular in Cambodia) with eleven heads and eleven pairs of arms.

She appeared, over time, in Japan, Java, Cambodia, China, and Tibet. However, the Tibetans had already fallen in love with Tārā, so her cult never gained great popularity there. It was in India, above all, that the goddess Prajñāpāramitā manifested. There was even a great statue of her on the Vulture's Peak at Rajgir, where the Buddha gave so many discourses.

India being the centre of devotion to Prajñāpāramitā, when the Muslims trampled Buddhism underfoot in that country, her cult largely disappeared. As the Muslims systematically destroyed the monasteries, smashed statues, and burned books, the Wisdom goddess went into hiding.

It is really only in the twentieth century, and due largely to the work of one man, that the goddess is once again displaying her face in so many different lands. The life's work of the German scholar Edward Conze was to translate virtually all the Perfection of Wisdom texts into English. Thanks to his efforts the goddess moves freely among us once more.

Though the cult of Prajñāpāramitā survived and continued outside India, so weakened had it become that after extensive research Edward Conze could catalogue fewer than fifty icons of her in existence. Since then, at least one more has come to light. A few years ago a film crew went to Tholing in western Tibet to record the extraordinary temple paintings there. They had been neglected, and some were so covered in dust as to be unrecognizable. The crew filmed the dust being carefully removed from an anonymous mural. As the picture was cleaned in front of it, the camera recorded the apparition of an exquisite golden goddess.

Emblems of the Wisdom goddess

In her different manifestations, Prajñāpāramitā is shown with various symbols or emblems. There are six main ones, and we shall perhaps come to understand our Wisdom goddess better if we look briefly at each of them in turn.

(1) The lotus. The lotus is a symbol for that which transcends the mundane. So, although we have been speaking of her as a goddess and of meeting her in the archetypal realm, it is clear that Prajñāpāramitā is essentially a manifestation of the *dharmakāya*.

The lotus is also a symbol of spiritual receptivity. To 'understand' the Perfection of Wisdom we have to be prepared to stand under it, and learn from it. In doing so we may even have to accept that we do not know anything about anything, spiritual or mundane! This is, in a sense, the message of the *Heart Sūtra* – that our experience is ungraspable, and even the concepts of Buddhism do not capture the truth of things. At best they are only 'fingers pointing to the moon'.

(2) The book. Her association with the book emphasizes that Prajñāpāramitā embodies the wisdom of all the books in the Perfect Wisdom corpus. The book also represents the fact that, although we aspire to go beyond words and concepts, most of us cannot just ignore culture and learning. We need to train and develop our rational faculty, not try to

dispense with it. Once we have fully trained our intellect, then we can turn it to the Perfection of Wisdom, and let it discover for itself its inadequacy in apprehending Reality. The rational mind has to be developed to a point where it can see through itself – acknowledge its own limitations.

(3) The vajra. It may seem strange for a gentle goddess to wield such a weapon – though Athena, another wisdom goddess, is also a warrior. Transcendental wisdom is both soft and hard. It is soft in the sense that it is subtle and elusive. If you try to grasp it directly you will always fail. It comes to you gently, from the side, as it were – from a 'direction' you cannot cover. Because of that it is hard in the sense that it cannot be parried. It smashes to pieces all our mundane ideas about reality. Thus Perfect Wisdom has a destructive aspect, which the diamond thunderbolt well symbolizes.

(4) The sword. The flaming sword is an attribute of Mañjuśrī – the Prince of Wisdom. Mañjuśrī and Prajñāpāramitā represent two methods of approach to the goal of wisdom, so it is not surprising that they should share certain symbols.

(5) The mālā. A mālā (Tibetan *trhengwa* – literally 'garland') is what in the West would be called a rosary. In Buddhism it is used for counting mantras and other practices. Its association with Prajñāpāramitā suggests the importance of repetition for arriving at wisdom. In the West especially, where novelty is the great goddess, we tend to flit from one experience to another. All too often having done, or read, something once, or at most a few times, we feel we have drunk the experience to the dregs. Novelty lives on the surface of life, but Perfect Wisdom is preserved in the depths.

To achieve wisdom through the Perfection of Wisdom texts we have to read them repeatedly (some of the sūtras reiterate themselves – eighty-per-cent of the *Perfection of Wisdom in 100,000 Lines* consists of repetitions.) We need to meditate repeatedly on the same themes of emptiness and impermanence. It is only with this devoted, loving return to the same sources of inspiration that we shall gradually deepen our insight, shall come to understand the same sūtras and subjects in ever-deepening ways. Prajñāpāramitā does not reveal all her secrets at a first meeting. To woo her successfully we have to be faithful to her.

(6) The begging-bowl. This is the utensil of the wanderering Buddhist monk or nun. It symbolizes the movement away from worldly ties. It implies the need for renunciation if we are to find Perfect Wisdom. We may not physically leave our home and our country, but in the search for Wisdom we shall have to be prepared to give up our old cramped self and our conventional ideas about the world.

The visualization of Prajñāpāramitā

We have seen that Prajñāpāramitā appears in a number of forms, and can have various symbolic attributes. Naturally, then, there are various traditional ways of visualizing her. Geshe Kelsang Gyatso describes a practice in which she is visualized in connection with recitation of the *Heart Sūtra*.[12] This practice was used in Tibet for warding off hindrances – especially the four Māras. These are personifications of all the negative forces – internal and external – that hinder our quest for Enlightenment.

The *Sādhanamālā*, a very important Indian collection of visualization practices, gives nine different sādhanas of Prajñāpāramitā. Rather than examining a sādhana in detail, we shall look at part of one of these visualizations. It begins with a series of magical transformations that take place within the blue sky of Emptiness.

First, on a lotus and moon in front of us, appears the syllable *dhīḥ*. This is the seed syllable particularly associated with transcendental wisdom. We have already met it in the mantra of Mañjuśrī. The seed syllable shines in the blueness, made of golden-yellow light.

Next we see a book of the Perfection of Wisdom. It is usually visualized not as a bound volume but in the form that one finds in Tibetan monasteries. The leaves of the manuscript are sandwiched loose between covers – like a thick book with no spine. They are then wrapped in silk. Perhaps in the future, Western meditators will see it as an ancient, leather-bound volume.

Then on a full-blown lotus appears Prajñāpāramitā herself. So the sequence of the visualization is first the seed syllable, then the book, and finally the goddess. It is as though the practice recapitulates the whole development of Perfect Wisdom in human consciousness. First there is just the blue sky, the experience of Emptiness itself. Then the seed appears – a communication of Wisdom on the most subtle of levels. Next the teaching is put into words, into the Perfection of Wisdom literature. Finally it appears again, transfigured into a golden goddess.

This goddess is seated on a blue lotus and a white moon mat. She is not sixteen years old like the Bodhisattvas; she is much more mature than that, though still very beautiful. Wisdom is something that takes time to ripen. Prajñāpāramitā is often described as 'the mother of all the Buddhas'. She is mature in having given birth to countless Buddhas. Prajñāpāramitā represents the realization of śūnyatā, and there is no other way to gain Enlightenment. As the *Heart Sūtra* has it,

> A Bodhisattva, through having relied on the perfection of wisdom, dwells without thought-coverings. In the absence of thought-coverings he has not been made to tremble, he has overcome what can upset, and in the end he attains to nirvāṇa.[13]

It is Perfect Wisdom which gives birth to Buddhahood. Prajñāpāramitā is said to regard the Buddhas like a mother fondly watching her children at play. She wears a tiara with jewels of the five colours. These embody the wisdoms of the five Buddhas. Her hands are placed in the mudrā of teaching the Dharma. She holds the stems of two lotuses, which open out into pale-blue blossoms, one at each shoulder.[14] As always, upon each of them is a white moon mat. On each moon mat lies a book of the Perfection of Wisdom.

There is just one more very striking feature of the goddess. We have said that she is golden yellow in colour. However, if we look closely we shall see that the golden-yellow light from her body is given off by millions of Buddhas. Her whole body is made up of golden Buddhas. It is as though the goddess of the Perfection of Wisdom is a great galaxy. Seen from afar, the galaxy is in the most pleasing shape imaginable. Coming closer, we see that it comprises endless Enlightened Beings: constellations of Buddhas, starry multitudes of Awakened Ones.

Then light emanates from the centre of the galaxy, from the heart of Prajñāpāramitā. Down the light ray comes the mantra of the Wisdom goddess: *oṃ āḥ dhīḥ hūṃ svāhā*. It enters your heart and begins to echo there, bestowing wisdom on you through another of its transformations.

The mantra *oṃ āḥ dhīḥ hūṃ svāhā* which is used in this sādhana conveys the message of the Prajñāpāramitā literature, but through the medium of symbolic sound. It is one of three mantras commonly associated with the Perfection of Wisdom. It is not readily translatable, appealing only to a level of the psyche that does not trade in words.[15] The other two common mantras can be given some rational explanation.

First there is the mantra *gate gate pāragate pārasaṃgate bodhi svāhā*.[16] This comes at the end of the *Heart Sūtra*, and is more generally associated with the Perfection of Wisdom literature than with the Wisdom goddess, though it does appear in some of her sādhanas. It has been translated by Edward Conze as 'Gone, gone, gone beyond, gone altogether beyond, O what an awakening, all hail!' The mantra symbolizes a deepening apprehension of Reality. According to one tradition, its first four words correspond to the four levels of śūnyatā. The first *gate* (pronounced *gutt-ay*) symbolizes going beyond saṃsāra. The second represents the emptiness of the concept of nirvāṇa, especially the view of Enlightenment as something distinct or separate from the phenomenal world. With *pāragate* one realizes the emptiness of all distinctions, and in particular that between saṃsāra and nirvāṇa. With *pārasaṃgate* one goes beyond all concepts whatsoever, even letting drop the idea of śūnyatā. Gelukpa lamas relate these four words to the first four of the Mahāyāna paths, and *bodhi* or *bodhi svāhā* to the fifth.[17]

Secondly there is the homage found at the beginning of the *Heart Sūtra*, which can be repeated as a mantra: *oṃ namo bhagavatyai āryaprajñāpāramitāyai*. Edward Conze translates this as 'Homage to the Perfection of Wisdom, the Lovely, the Holy'. The *gate gate* mantra, with its association with the four levels of śūnyatā, might appeal to those more intellectually inclined, whereas this invocation is an outpouring of faith and devotion to the goddess. It is characteristic of Buddhism that it should provide such differing paths to the goal.

Regularly performing a sādhana of Prajñāpāramitā produces an ever-deepening involvement with the Wisdom goddess. To start with, the goddess becomes a focus for devotion. For men, her practice can often absorb the romantic and other feelings that might be evoked by meeting a beautiful, mature woman. For women, she is often a figure with which to identify, the most positive of all role models. Thus for both sexes energy can easily be engaged by the meditation, and hence poured into the contemplation of Wisdom.

If this process continues, the practice enters the realm of the archetypal. In Jungian terms, a man may project the highest aspect of his anima, while a woman may encounter the Magna Mater. She becomes for the meditator the archetypal Wisdom goddess found in many traditions. For the Gnostics she was Sophia, for the Greeks Athena. She is found in the Tarot as the High Priestess, who holds a scroll – corresponding to the book of Prajñāpāramitā. She is seated between two pillars – one light, one dark. Imbibing her knowledge will enable you to pass between the pillars and transcend all dichotomies.

Prajñāpāramitā is the Wisdom goddess of India – once described as staggeringly beautiful to the point of being scorching. Her meditation can become a way of experiencing the archetypal beauty of the refined levels of one's mind. Finally, with faithful practice, she can become far more than that. She can become the experience of transcendental wisdom itself – the transcendence of the world of subject and object.

Anyone who reaches this level will truly begin travelling in realms of gold. They will be carried up to a fresh vantage point, a new peak of their being. From that pinnacle they will see not a new ocean or a new planet, but a new reality. They will be reborn out of the infinite creativity of the Wisdom goddess, and will add their brilliance to the galaxy of golden Buddhas.

Vajrasattva

Three

Vajrasattva – Prince of Purity

In meeting Vajrasattva (Tibetan *Dorje Sempa*) in this chapter, we are encountering for the first time a Buddha who does not appear in the Mahāyāna sūtras, only in the tantras. He is a rather mysterious, even esoteric, figure, who plays a number of important roles in Tantric practice.

Sometimes he appears as a kind of reflex of the deep blue, immutable Buddha, Akṣobhya. At other times he appears as the '*adi*-Buddha' – pure white, naked and unadorned, in sexual embrace with a white female partner. *Adi* means from the beginning or primordial. This does not mean he has existed since the beginning of creation – Buddhism does not think in those terms. The adi-Buddha does not appear at a first point in time, he transcends time altogether. He represents the potential of the mind to transcend the continuum of time and space, a potential that is always available to us. When you emerge beyond these limitations of consciousness, you find you are Enlightened. Not only that; beyond time, you find you have always been Enlightened. In your essential nature you have always been a 'diamond being', have always been Vajrasattva.

This diamond nature, outside time, is totally pure. It has never been sullied or stained by any of your actions within time. Hence Vajrasattva represents the beginningless purity of your deepest nature. The path to Enlightenment of the devotee of Vajrasattva, then, is a path of ever-increasing purification.

One of the most important sets of meditation practices in the Tantra, used in slightly varying forms by all schools of Tibetan Buddhism, is known as the *mūla*, or Foundation, Yogas.[18] These are often performed as preliminaries to the practice of Highest Tantra (*anuttarayoga*), and are in themselves extremely effective methods of self-transformation.

The first, according to a common Nyingma classification,[19] is Going for Refuge and Prostrations. This involves visualizing a vast assembly of Buddhas, Bodhisattvas, and other symbols of the transcendental path, and reciting a formula committing yourself to attain Enlightenment. At the same time you make full-length prostrations on the ground, and imagine all living beings reciting and prostrating with you. This recitation and prostration is repeated 100,000 times over a period of months or years. Performed wholeheartedly, this practice greatly deepens your commitment to following the Buddhist path to its endless end.

The aim of the second practice is the development of the Bodhicitta, the cosmic will to Enlightenment. Again, there is a verse to be recited 100,000 times. By the time this is completed, you know that you can never be satisfied with making your own escape from the prison of saṃsāra. You are now committed to engineering a 'mass breakout' – to helping all living beings to attain Enlightenment.

Out of the first two mūla yogas comes the determination to gain Enlightenment as fast as possible, so as to help all living creatures who have been circling in saṃsāra since beginningless time. But, according to Buddhist tradition, you too have been taking rebirth since beginningless time, and in all those lives, being unenlightened, you have presumably been piling up unskilful deeds, which hinder you from gaining Enlightenment. How on earth can you ever purify yourself?

It is here that Vajrasattva comes to your rescue. The third Foundation Yoga involves repeatedly visualizing Vajrasattva and reciting his mantra – once again until the number of recitations reaches 100,000. This practice is a very deep purification of all levels of your being – body, speech, and mind.

It is very important to understand how this purification works. The purificatory practice is not of the same order as the unskilfulness which it purifies. (After all, if that were the case, since you have been heaping up hindrances since beginningless time it would take endless aeons to purify them.) On the contrary, Vajrasattva's purification comes about through the realization that in your deepest nature you were never impure.

Your true Vajrasattva nature is beyond time and space. It is primordially pure because it is on a level of 'existence' to which karma does not apply. That is why it can purify all your karma.[20]

Sādhanas of purification of Vajrasattva are much used in the Tantra. They are performed as part of the Foundation Yogas, and frequently as a daily practice. They are also used to repair infractions of vows, whether the Bodhisattva ordination vows or the Tantric *samaya* – the vows taken during Tantric initiation. There are many such sādhanas, though the differences between them are relatively superficial.

In sādhanas of purification, Vajrasattva is usually visualized as white in colour, though different sādhanas may specify slightly different forms. In some he holds a vajra to his heart and a bell at his left hip or knee, in others he holds the vajra and bell crossed. In some he is a single figure, in others he appears in the form known as Heruka Vajrasattva, embracing his white Tantric consort.

There are other sādhanas of Vajrasattva in which he may appear in other colours. Frequently he is a deep or sapphire blue. I know of devotees who visualize a yellow form. You also find mandalas of Vajrasattvas of the same five colours as the Buddhas: white, yellow, red, blue, and green. However, we shall concentrate here on a form of Vajrasattva meditation which is used for purification, as it is in this context, as a purifier of faults and negative karma, that he is most commonly invoked.

A sādhana of purification

For this purification meditation to be most effective, it needs to be prefaced by a period of reflection in which we make a frank appraisal of our shortcomings. The path of purification begins with acceptance of the *need* for purification. Vajrasattva can only purify us to the extent that we honestly recognize how far we have strayed away from his diamond light. The more wholeheartedly we admit to what stands in our way on the path to Buddhahood, the more complete will be the purification. Here we are not concerned with beating our breasts, wanting to atone for

Heruka Vajrasattva

the offence our sins have caused to some external deity. We just make an honest assessment of our own inadequacies, failings, or even evil, and regret the suffering we have caused ourselves and others. This is done in the context of the understanding that the beauty and strength of Vajrasattva is *our* beauty and strength, from which our negative actions have estranged us.

That done, we allow everything around us to dissolve into a vast blue sky. Its infinite freedom stretches away in all directions. All our hopes and fears, our chains of thoughts, vanish into the blueness. Everything is still.

Above our heads, out of the blue emptiness, flowers a perfect white lotus. Above it is a circle of white light, a moon mat. On this spotless throne appears a figure made of white light. He is seated serenely in full-lotus posture, wearing dazzling silks and jewels made by craftsmen in light.

His right hand is held to his heart, palm upwards. Balanced perfectly upright upon it is a vajra, the diamond sceptre of the Enlightened Ones. The vajra may appear as gold or crystal. Whatever its semblance it is made of light, of Mind, of Reality itself.

His left hand is at his left side, holding a vajra-bell (Sanskrit *vajraghaṇṭā*) – a silver bell with a vajra handle. His head is crowned with a diadem of five jewels, and his body is surrounded by an aura of five-coloured light: white, yellow, red, blue, and green – symbolizing that Vajrasattva is the union of the mandala of the five Buddhas, the complete embodiment of their wisdoms. He has long black hair flowing over his shoulders, and he looks down at us with a smile that transforms our universe. It is a gaze of total acceptance.

At his heart's core is another small white lotus and moon mat. On this, standing upright, is the deep-blue seed syllable *hūṃ*. Around it is a circlet of white letters, like a string of pearls. These are the letters of the 'hundred syllable mantra' of Vajrasattva.

As we deepen our concentration on the radiant figure above us, we see dewdrops of white light-nectar forming on the *hūṃ* and the white mantra garland. These drops become heavier, fuller. Slowly they begin to fall. They flow down through the vacuous body of Vajrasattva and kiss the crown of our head. The nectar drops are very cool, very soothing, very healing. They flow into our body, drop by glistening drop. We feel more deeply refreshed than a thirsty nomad at an oasis spring.

The rhythm of the falling nectar quickens. The descending drops are no longer distinguishable. They become a flowing, curative stream, pouring from Vajrasattva's heart into our body and mind. The light-stream begins washing away all our unskilful karma, all our foolish actions, all our selfishness. Even physical diseases are cleansed away. Clouds of darkness fall from us.

The purification is reinforced by the turning of the letters in Vajrasattva's heart. They dance gently around the *hūṃ*, chanting the sound of the mantra: *oṃ vajrasattva samayam*.... One by one the hundred syllables restore us to our true home, reconcile us to our true nature.

The glistening light-nectar cleanses us of even our flesh-and-blood nature, born to die. Our body becomes like a perfect crystal vase. This body-shaped light-vase is completely filled with the white nectar. We feel light, pure, and free as the blue sky.

There is more to the sādhana, but perhaps this is enough to enable you to get an inkling of the sense of release and purification that successful practice of the sādhana brings about.

In Tantric circles, this sādhana is known to be very strong medicine with far-reaching effects. It purifies body, speech, and mind. It is not unusual for there to be physical side-effects from its performance.

Vajrasattva is sometimes referred to in the Tantra as the one who saves from hell. This is no doubt partly because his sādhana is used for repairing broken Tantric vows. (Neglecting to keep the Tantric vows is considered very unskilful karma, which will have unpleasant consequences.) His meditation is considered to be particularly efficacious as a preparation for death, or when performed on behalf of someone who has died.

The meditation is a very good antidote to irrational guilt, or self-hatred. It is effective in overcoming unhelpful self-views which, sadly, people sometimes pick up from some aspects of their Christian conditioning. Through this meditation you can realize that you are not a 'miserable sinner', but pure in your essential nature. In contrast to the doctrine of original sin, Tantric Buddhism asserts original purity – an unquenchable purity that has lain hidden since beginningless time. In meeting Vajrasattva you find once again the indestructible, pure essence of the mind.

Vajrasattva as spiritual protector

In the case of some Buddhas and Bodhisattvas there is, as we have seen, a particular myth or archetypal pattern that serves as an approach to experiencing them. For Vajrasattva that myth is the myth of the return journey. A story in the *Saddharma Puṇḍarīka* gives a good example of this. A young man leaves his father's house and wanders from place to place, finding work where he can. Over the years he travels to many distant countries, but he is always poor, surviving on the most menial work. Meanwhile, his father has been amassing a great fortune, and longs to find his son and share his happiness with him.

After many years the son in his wanderings comes upon a great mansion with a man sitting outside displaying his wealth in the ostentatious Indian fashion. He starts to move away, but the rich man – who is of course his father – sees him in the crowd. Though his son does not recognize him, his father recognizes him at once. He sends messengers hurrying after him, but the son assumes he is in trouble, and evades them.

At this point the rich man realizes that his son has become so used to his low status that he is deeply scared of the rich and famous. So he sends servants, dressed in old clothes, to see his son. They offer him a job, just working in the grounds of the mansion. The son accepts. His first task is to clear away a large mound of earth. Gradually, though, he is promoted until he becomes used to entering the mansion. His promotion continues until finally he becomes the rich man's steward and treasurer, accustomed to handling his great wealth. Only at that point does the rich man reveal that his steward is his lost son, and that the fortune he is administering is his own inheritance.

The myth of Vajrasattva is echoed in all stories in which the hero or heroine is lost and finally returns to their homeland. We are all alienated from our essential nature, and hence wander through the world believing ourselves poor and worthless. Through the practice of Vajrasattva, we contact our true nature, our spiritual inheritance, and become possessed of riches beyond our dreams.

This movement from alienation to discovering and identifying with our true nature is exemplified by the developing movement within the 'hundred syllable mantra' of Vajrasattva.[21]

The mantra begins: *oṃ vajrasattva samayam anupālaya* – 'Om Vajrasattva! Preserve the bond!' The word *samaya* means bond, or contract. When you are initiated into the practice of a particular Buddha or Bodhisattva, it is as though there is an agreement made. You for your part agree to perform the practice faithfully, to invoke the Enlightened experience regularly in the form of that particular Buddha or Bodhisattva. The Enlightened Mind for its part – and of course we are speaking metaphorically here – agrees to bestow on you the fruits of the practice.

So it is as though, before we begin the mantra, we are in a state of alienation from our essential nature. This alienation is usually experienced emotionally. Vajrasattva's shining figure may appear mysterious, distant, even cold and aloof, like some far-off snow peak. However, through recalling our bond with Vajrasattva, we realize that we are linked to him, a connection exists between us and Enlightenment, and through spiritual practice we can close that gap.

Vajrasattvatvenopatiṣṭa – 'As Vajrasattva stand before me.' Here we begin to see that, however far we may have strayed away from it, we are in a sense still protected by our diamond nature. We begin to see Vajrasattva as a spiritual friend. We realize that in the depths of our being is a tremendous spiritual power which, if summoned, will come to our aid. We could see the mantra as a magic spell. With it we conjure Enlightenment to appear before us in the form of Vajrasattva.

Alternatively, *upatiṣṭa* could be translated 'stand by me'. This suggests an image of being in a battle, surrounded by enemies, and losing ground. At the end of your strength you remember that long ago, you cannot recall when, a great hero vowed that if you called on him he would come to protect you. So you invoke Vajrasattva. The next thing you know, a diamond warrior has appeared from nowhere, standing shoulder to shoulder with you.

Dṛḍho me bhava – 'Be firm for me.' He covers your weaknesses. At the sight of him, eyes cool and clear, dauntless and resourceful, your attackers fall back. He is that higher aspect of yourself which will always stand firm, unshakeable as the diamond thunderbolt in his hand.

Sutoṣyo me bhava, supoṣyo me bhava, anurakto me bhava – 'Be greatly pleased for me. Deeply nourish me. Love me passionately.' Now the relationship becomes much closer. Vajrasattva is no longer a distant protector; he has become an intimate friend. His radiance has become a white fire, melting with its love everything that keeps you standing cold and aloof from truth.

Sarva siddhiṃ me prayaccha, sarva karmasu ca me cittaṃ śreyaḥ kuru hūṃ – 'Grant me *siddhi* in all things, and in all actions make my mind most excellent. *Hūṃ*.' The relationship between you is now so close that Vajrasattva can have a deeply transforming influence on you. With these lines you open yourself completely to him.

Ha ha ha ha hoḥ – Having confessed and let go of everything negative which distanced you from Vajrasattva, the last millimetres of separation from him disappear. You become Vajrasattva, eternally pure, and as soon as you do so you see that you have always been Vajrasattva, pure and Enlightened since beginningless time. The joy and release of this experience is expressed in a peal of laughter that echoes through eternity. The five syllables of that laughter represent total penetration of the wisdoms of the five Buddhas.

Bhagavan sarva tathāgatavajra mā me muñca – 'Blessed one! Vajra of all the Tathāgatas! Do not abandon me.' Vajrasattva is the vajra of all the Tathāgatas, inasmuch as he represents the primordial purity and intuitive realization of śūnyatā which is the essence of all Enlightened experience. Having gained the Enlightened perspective of Vajrasattva, not only do you realize your essential unity with the insight of all the Buddhas, you also see clearly that the essential nature of all beings is also pure and empty. To emphasize this, in some Vajrasattva sādhanas you visualize all other sentient beings being transformed into Vajrasattva, just as you have been.

Vajri bhava mahāsamayasattva āḥ – 'Be the vajra bearer, being of the great bond! *āḥ*.' Under certain circumstances the syllables *hūṃ phaṭ* are added to the end of the mantra. They are not really translatable. The *hūṃ* is usually appended when the mantra is being recited for the benefit of someone who has died. The *phaṭ* is considered by Tibetan tradition to be efficacious for subduing demons.[22]

Looking at the mantra section by section, we see that it recapitulates the myth of the journey home to rediscover our essential nature. In this way it follows the typical Tantric procedure of taking the goal as the path. Through what begins as an imaginative union with your Vajrasattva nature, your innate purity, you come to discover that purity directly.

Vajrasattva's purity

We have seen that contacting Vajrasattva through his visualization and mantra recitation leads us towards an experience of primordial purity. It is this experience which Vajrasattva promises us as his side of the *samaya* bond. We can help him to help us by considering the characteristics of purity.

We talk of many things as pure. Young children (at least pre-Freud) were thought to be pure; virgins are pure. We also speak of pure alcohol when it is 175 degrees proof (in the UK, 200 degrees in the American system). Sometimes purity is associated with naivety, or even with a rather anaemic goodness. So it is important, if we are to develop a strong emotional connection with Vajrasattva, that we recognize the qualities of his purity. In this section we shall consider two of them.

The first quality of purity particularly appropriate to Vajrasattva is that when something is pure it is unadulterated. It is not diluted or watered down, not mixed with anything extraneous or inessential. This kind of purity certainly is not weak. You only have to think of the phrase 'pure dynamite'....

In trying to unite with Vajrasattva we are aspiring to become a vajra being. We are trying to experience ourselves, our consciousness, at full strength, completely concentrated, essential. To unite with him we need to live in a way that is 'full strength', totally authentic, with all the inessentials – everything weakening or diluting – thrown away. It is something of these qualities that is suggested by Vajrasattva sometimes appearing naked and unadorned. This kind of purity, of true, authentic being, has nothing weak about it.

In this sense, too, Vajrasattva represents pure unadulterated consciousness, a mind not diluted by chasing after its reflections in mundane experience. Our minds usually move outwards toward sense-experience, and in this way the brilliant light of consciousness is dissipated. Vajrasattva's white intensity is a symbol of the experience of a mind totally focused, absorbed in the contemplation of Reality, just as Vajrasattva holds the diamond-sceptre of Reality to his heart. It is this pure, undifferentiated experience that is true purity.

This line of thought perhaps explains Vajrasattva's special connection with death. Death is the time when our past actions, skilful or unskilful, rise up in our minds. Our future rebirth is determined by our skilful and unskilful karmas.[23] Thus death is the time when the need to purify our negative karma becomes most apparent.

More than this, at death consciousness is withdrawn from the body and its senses. It is as though the expanding universe of consciousness – tending to scatter itself in all directions amongst sensory experience – had reversed its trend. The mind once again focuses itself into an ever-increasing intensity. In the *Tibetan Book of the Dead* this centripetal movement of consciousness is said to culminate in the experience of the 'Clear Light of Reality'. For a brief moment undifferentiated consciousness shines, subjectless and objectless. Usually this experience is too much for us, and consciousness at once begins objectifying itself again, in the forms of the visions of the bardo. You could say that Vajrasattva represents the experience of that totally concentrated consciousness, the encounter with the clear light when it is accepted, when instead of running from it, you hold that experience to your heart.

The second quality of things that are pure is that they are new, fresh, unstained by experience. Advertisers talk of pure new wool, for example.

The experience of purity is the experience of newness. Purification is always purification of the past. If you succeed in purifying yourself completely, then, in a sense, you have no past. To become a vajra being, you have to try to see everything as new, including yourself. This is the final stage of purification. You forget about whatever you did that needed cleansing, and you begin anew.

In practising the third Foundation Yoga, and reciting the Vajrasattva mantra 100,000 times, one of my strongest experiences was of the freshness and newness of the world into which the meditation led me. I could see why, when he is not seen as a sixth Buddha, or *adi*-Buddha, Vajrasattva is regarded as a kind of reflex form of Akṣobhya, the Buddha of the East. Not only do they share the vajra as their emblem. Akṣobhya is associated with dawn – the dawn of a new day, a fresh morning, a unique arising of the light of the world.

This newness aspect of purity again relates to Vajrasattva's association with death. It is only with the death of the old that the new can be born. The old, stale personality dies and in its place appears a Vajrasattva, completely spontaneous, because every moment is new.

Vajra as 'what is'

Vajrasattva sits serenely holding the vajra to his heart. His left hand clasps the vajra handle of a bell. The bell is usually said to symbolize wisdom; the vajra symbolizes skilful means (Sanskrit *upāya*) – the infinite ways in which an Enlightened One, out of compassion, shares his wisdom with the world. Together the vajra and bell symbolize the fusion of all polarities, including masculine and feminine qualities, in one Enlightened experience.

The vajra also represents Reality. In the Tantra things are given the prefix 'vajra' to remind you of their essential nature, which is Emptiness. In a Tantric ritual you might offer not a flower, but a vajra-flower, not incense but vajra-incense. Even the most ugly or disgusting experiences are 'vajra' for the Tantra. In this way, everyday experiences are seen as expressions or manifestations of one non-dual Reality.

However, to begin with at least, this explanation of vajra as Reality will be somewhat abstract. It will not really move us. So how can we begin to approach the experience of vajra on the level at which we find ourselves at present? Perhaps a good starting point would be just to think of vajra as 'the facts', just as what is actually happening. Vajra is what is. Vajra is what has happened, so there is no point in arguing with it. Vajra is whatever is taking place right now – so there is no sense in denying it.

I mean this on a quite simple, everyday level. It may not seem very exalted, or spiritual. However, if we look at our lives, we find that we spend much of our time arguing with what has happened or what is going on. There might be a large pile of washing-up squatting by our sink, and we don't want to do it. We never liked the shape of our nose, and wish it were different, and so on.

I had a useful experience a few years ago, when I was learning karate. As well as teaching us techniques, the *sensei*, or instructor, also ensured that we did plenty of fitness exercises. There was one particular combination of exercises: so many jumps with knees to the chest, so many press-ups, and other things, that I found particularly excruciating. All through the class I was dreading the moment when the *sensei* would launch us into this painful and exhausting sequence.

When the awful moment came, I would sometimes do it complaining to myself; at others I would try to adopt a positive attitude. One day I realized that all this was wasted effort. The simple fact was that sometime during the class I would just do so many press-ups, etc. I could complain to myself, sulk, scheme, go numb, be exultant, or even manic. It made little difference. I would still be there, sweating my way through the sequence. The easiest way to do it was just to do it.

It is a good beginning to see vajra as objective reality in this quite basic way – just as 'the facts', what is happening. If you really accept things in this way then craving and aversion disappear. You waste no energy. I found just doing the karate exercises was even easier than trying to be positive about them.

If we accept things in this simple, everyday way, then, in a sense, everything becomes perfect. A grey, rainy day is a perfectly grey, rainy day. A leper is a perfect leper, a corpse a perfect corpse. Ego could be defined as 'the non-acceptance of things as they are'. Ceasing to fight objective reality is a movement beyond ego.

Vajrasattva holds the vajra to his heart. He accepts things as they really are. Therefore, for him, they are perfectly pure. He accepts you as you are. He sees you as perfect. That is why he can purify all your faults. As Seng Tsan, the third patriarch of Zen, wrote in his *Affirming Faith in Mind*, 'The Great Way is not difficult for those who do not pick and choose.'[24]

In talking about accepting 'the facts', things as they are, I am not advocating passivity. Unless you begin by accepting what is, you cannot change it. Accepting things as they are is a powerful, active experience, simple and direct. Through doing this you become one with life, and then you can really help to transform it. Until then, you are standing apart from it. This practice of not fighting what is there is the spiritual equivalent of grasping the nettle. To become one with Vajrasattva, to become a vajra being, you have to take up the vajra and hold it to your heart. That involves giving up hopes, expectations, and fantasies. You even have to relinquish ideas of what is perfect and imperfect. Then everything will be perfect, just as it is. Everything will be pure.

The path of Vajrasattva, the path of purity, begins with acceptance of what has happened. We have to accept objectively all our failures, our unskilful thoughts, words, and acts – even, perhaps, our wickedness. We accept who we are at present. This becomes very much easier to do once we have faith that in our deepest nature we are still completely pure. Relying on the *samaya*, the link we have made, we call on that secret diamond nature.

The response is instantaneous. The smiling figure of Vajrasattva, our spiritual protector, rains down healing nectar upon us. Through reciting his mantra we steadily close the gap between him and us. Finally, we *are* Vajrasattva, holding the diamond sceptre of Reality to our heart. The last fact that we have to accept is that we are eternally Enlightened, beyond space and time. We are, and have always been, completely pure.

Padmasambhava

Four

The Esoteric Buddha and the Lotus-Born Guru

For 2,500 years Buddhists have considered with awe the achievement of Siddhārtha Gautama. What induces such tremendous respect in them is not just that he gained Enlightenment, but that he did so without a teacher. (He learned meditation from Ārāḍa Kālāma and Udraka Rāmapūtra, but neither of them could show him the way to escape from suffering – *that* he had to discover unaided.) Contemplating the difficulties that the Buddha had to overcome has given Buddhism a very great appreciation of the value of a spiritual teacher.

As Buddhism developed, and the three *yānas* unfolded, the role and significance of the spiritual teacher changed. In the first two *yānas* the teacher may act as a preceptor, responsible for introducing you to the Buddha way, or as a *kalyāṇa mitra* – a spiritual friend. The *kalyāṇa mitra* is like an older brother or sister in the Dharma, who helps, advises, and encourages.

In the Vajrayāna, the teacher transforms into the *vajraguru*. The relationship with a Tantric teacher is a *samaya*, or bond, at least as binding as that between the meditator and the Buddha or Bodhisattva that he or she visualizes. In Tantra it is said that all blessings spring from the guru. The relationship is more like that of a doctor with a patient who desperately wants a cure and has total belief in the doctor's method.

The guru is a vajraguru partly because everything in the Tantra is vajra – everything is seen as an expression of the ineffable Reality of which the vajra is the chief Tantric symbol. The vajra prefix implies that the guru embodies Reality. He may formally teach the Dharma or he may not. However, just what he is expresses Reality. His being and mode of living are themselves a teaching. For his disciple, the communication of the Tantric guru may come as a thunderbolt. The vajraguru is spiritually ruthless. He is the teacher who will stop at nothing to awaken his disciple from the slumber of saṃsāra. There are many stories in the Tantra, as in Zen, of gurus using drastic methods to get through to their disciples.

For the Tantric disciple, the guru's kindness can never be repaid. Through initiation the guru bestows practices which can propel the student rapidly to Buddhahood. The guru is the source, the fountainhead, of all his or her development. In fact, for the Tantra, particularly Highest Tantra, the guru is a Buddha.

Ideally the guru should be Enlightened. Tantric initiation partly symbolizes the empowering of a far-advanced Bodhisattva with the full qualities of an Awakened One. Most gurus fall a long way short of full Enlightenment. Nonetheless, the Tantra is concerned with finding correlates in actual experience for the highest values of the spiritual path. As we saw in Chapter One, it says, in effect, 'If you are not in direct contact with a Buddha, who in your present experience comes closest to that level?' The answer is, of course, your guru. So the guru becomes what is called the 'esoteric' Buddha Refuge. It is esoteric not in the sense of secret, but because it is not an experience that everyone can share. It is only if you enter into a close, devoted relationship with a teacher that he begins to function as a Buddha Refuge for you.

It is also esoteric in the sense that it depends on an inner mental effort to see the guru in this way. Having received Tantric initiation from a teacher, the initiate is urged to make every effort to see the teacher as a fully Enlightened Buddha. He or she must disregard any apparent faults they may perceive in him or, rather, should attribute them to the impurity of their own mind.[25]

The Tantra holds firmly to the view that mind is king. If you see the guru as an ordinary person, you will receive the blessing of an ordinary person. If you see him as a Buddha, for you he will act as a Buddha, and your relationship with him will lead you quickly to Enlightenment.

Each school of Tibetan Buddhism has certain teachers whom it particularly reveres as the founders of its school, or for starting a particular lineage of teaching or initiation. Although they are historical figures, over the course of time they have taken on an archetypal significance. These teachers are frequently visualized, either during the practice of Guru Yoga or as part of the Refuge assemblies that we shall be looking at in Chapter Eight.

We shall now look briefly at a few of the most important of these gurus. (As usual, the number of figures one could describe is enormous.) We are going to begin by returning to the earliest sources of Tibetan Buddhism, to meet a figure who perhaps established an image of the vajraguru in the Tibetan mind, an image that helped to condition their understanding of the role of the Tantric guru in general. This is Padmasambhava ('lotus-born one'), known generally in Tibet as Guru Rimpoche ('precious guru'), and regarded as the founder of the Nyingma school of Tibetan Buddhism. We shall take him as an example of a vajraguru, describe some of his many forms, and say a little about how he can be meditated upon. This should convey something of the immense richness of symbolism and association surrounding these guru figures, built up over centuries of devotion. Padmasambhava is a particularly complex 'spiritual personality', but in principle I could have taken almost any of the other gurus described in this chapter as examples of the multifaceted nature of the guru in the Vajrayāna.

Padmasambhava – the lotus-born guru

Padmasambhava was instrumental in establishing Buddhism in Tibet in the eighth century. At that time King Trisong Detsen wanted to strengthen Buddhism, but was faced with fierce opposition from the Bonpos – followers of the indigenous shamanistic religion, led by a minister called Ma Zhang. A Buddhist abbot called Śāntarakṣita was persuaded to come from Nepal, but though he achieved a certain amount, he could not overcome the Bonpos single-handed. They had been using witchcraft against him, so he recommended that the king invite Padmasambhava who, as well as being a master of Buddhist scholarship, was also a *siddha*, an adept in the psychic powers engendered by Tantric meditation.

Padmasambhava came to Tibet, and the great monastery of Samye was built with his assistance. He is represented subduing the local deities of Tibet by his magic power, and binding them by oath to be servants and protectors of the Dharma.

There exists a truly extraordinary biography of Padmasambhava called *The Life and Liberation of Padmasambhava*. It describes how he is born as an emanation of the Buddha Amitābha, appearing spontaneously in a lotus on a lake in the country of Uḍḍiyāna. He is brought up by the king of that country as though he were his own son. Then, deciding it is time to leave the worldly life, he goes forth as a *bhikshu*. He studies all aspects of Buddhism, as well as medicine and astrology.

Next, he spends years meditating in all the great cremation grounds of India and the Himalayas. We are given graphic descriptions of the unspeakable horrors of these places. They are symbols for the endless fearful sufferings of conditioned existence itself. Yet in all these places Padmasambhava meditates unafraid, and converts the ḍākinīs – who, if you understand the text literally, are flesh-eating demonesses. In a cemetery called Mysterious Paths of Beatitude he is initiated by an Enlightened ḍākinī and receives supreme knowledge.

All through his life he is a controversial figure. On at least two occasions his flouting of convention causes such outrage that people attempt to burn him to death. Yet each time he emerges unscathed – rising phoenix-like from the flames. After performing his work of conversion in Tibet, he flies away to the land of the Rākṣasas (a race of ogres) to convert them too.

Padmasambhava's biography is of an unequalled richness. It is one of the great spiritual documents of mankind. Within it, inner and outer events are so fused that it is frequently impossible to decide on what level of reality the events described took place. Are we watching actual events in the outside world – events which to us seem preternatural? Are we reliving Padmasambhava's visionary experiences? Is he – are we – dreaming?

As presented in his life story, Padmasambhava becomes a kind of portmanteau figure – the embodiment in one person of all the accumulated knowledge, wisdom, love, and power of the Buddhist tradition. He is a master of all secular arts and sciences, as well as of all three *yānas* of Buddhism. In this way he represents the guru *par excellence*, for a guru prepares himself for his task of communicating the Dharma by first making himself a receptacle of the Buddhist tradition. From his teachers he receives the nectar of the Dharma, handed down from teacher to disciple ever since Śākyamuni managed to communicate it to Kauṇḍinya in the Deer Park at Sarnath.

I am reminded of a scene from an old Hollywood film, in which at a party of the rich and famous there was a great pyramid of champagne glasses. A liveried waiter arrived with a great bottle of champagne and kept pouring it into the top glass. When this was full it overflowed, and the bubbling liquid filled each tier of glasses, down and down in a foaming cascade. It is as though Śākyamuni Buddha is the top glass, who has made himself open to the transcendental. However, anyone who has absorbed the champagne brilliance of the Dharma cannot help but let it flow down to others. In this way, lineages of teaching are created. Padmasambhava represents the confluence of all these lineages – he is like a great crystal chalice in which all the bubbling streams of the Dharma meet.

His life is also a symbolic recapitulation of the spread of the teaching. His transformations are its new developments. In the course of his story he takes on numerous different forms, and at each stage, with each fresh metamorphosis, he acquires a new name. In this way he reminds us of two aspects of the guru. First, any guru worthy of the title has pursued his own development unremittingly. He has been prepared to undergo a number of spiritual deaths, and complete reorientations of consciousness, in his pursuit of the goal. The guru too, among his secondary characteristics, is a namer. In many cultures, entering a new stage of life entails a change of name. It is the guru who acts as guide as you enter upon the different stages of the spiritual path. Often, the guru will confer a new name upon you as you do so. This happens when you formally go for Refuge – when you ceremonially commit yourself to the Buddhist path. It happens if you leave home for the homeless life of a *bhikshu* or *bhikshuni*. It very often happens when you enter the mandala of the Vajrayāna. In order to name something you have to understand its true

Padmasambhava manifesting as Urgyen Dorje Chang

nature, its deeper significance. So in the Tantra the vajraguru introduces you to the level of consciousness embodied in the Tantric deities, and he names you – in a sense he tells you your *true* name, who you *really* are.

Padmasambhava has many forms, including an important set of eight which are frequently represented in Tantric art. First there is simply the form known as Padmasambhava. He sits wearing the three robes of the monk, and a red cap. Behind him to one side is a basket, a container representing the nourishment of the spiritual food of the Tripiṭaka (the 'three baskets' of the *sūtras*, the *vinaya*, and the *abhidharma*). In some representations he is given Tantric attributes, holding a vajra and skull cup, and with an adept's staff held at his left side.

Padmasambhava next manifests as Guru Śākya Senge ('lion of the Śākyas') or as Śākyamuni himself. In this form he appears in the way that Śākyamuni is usually represented: holding a begging-bowl, wearing the three yellow monastic robes, and golden yellow in complexion. Through this manifestation and the previous one he embodies the whole Buddhist tradition based on the sūtras. This form also emphasizes the fact that Padmasambhava is described as a 'second Buddha' by his devotees.[26]

Next, however, he appears as Urgyen Dorje Chang (also known as Tshokyi Dorje). In this form he is deep blue in colour, adorned with silks and jewels, holding a vajra and bell. He is locked in ecstatic sexual embrace with a consort, whose body is pure white. She holds a skull cup filled with ambrosia uplifted in her left hand. Here he embodies the whole Vajrayāna tradition, whose source is said to be Vajradhara (or Dorje Chang in Tibetan).

Now Padmasambhava transforms into Pema Gyalpo ('lotus king'). Here he is dressed like a king with a crown, jewels, and a turban. Around the turban is a diadem in which part of a wish-fulfilling gem can be seen. He sits relaxed in the posture of royal ease, holding a small Tantric double drum, known as a *damaru*, in his right hand, and a mirror in his left. His body is red in colour.

Another similar form appears, this time with natural skin colouring. He too wears royal attire and holds the damaru in his right hand. In his left he usually has a skull cup. In his belt is a *phurba*, a kind of magic dagger.

This is much used in Nyingma Tantric ritual. It was originally more like a peg or nail for pinning down demons and hindering psychic forces. It gradually became stylized into a three-edged blade ending in a point. The blade emerges from the body of a garuḍa. This implement embodies the power of a Tantric deity called Vajrakīla.[27] The phurba is often shown crowned with the head of Hayagrīva, a protector of the Dharma whom we shall encounter in Chapter Seven. The name of this manifestation is Lodan Choksey ('wise seeker of excellence').

Next, Padmasambhava enters the cremation ground, sits in meditation with his back to a stupa (or reliquary), and becomes Nyima Odzer ('sun-rays guru'). This is Padmasambhava as *siddha* and yogin. He wears only a loincloth of tiger skin, a meditation sash, and a crown of skulls. Yellow light radiates from his body. His hair, combed upwards, is crowned with a vajra. In his right hand he holds a trident staff. With his left hand he plays with the rays of the sun. This recalls an incident in his life story in which Padmasambhava caused the sun to halt in its tracks. He had made an agreement with a wine-seller to drink as much as he wanted and settle the bill at sunset. After seven days the sun still had not set. This is a good example of Tantric practice being bodied forth in legend. It has nothing whatever to do with alcohol. Rather it symbolizes Padmasambhava's entry into a state of consciousness in which time stands still, the mind and subtle psychic energies come to rest, and the yogin enjoys the *mahāsukha* – or Great Bliss – uninterruptedly.

The figures become wilder and more awe-inspiring. Next there appears a wrathful manifestation, Guru Senge Dradok ('one who teaches with a lion's voice'). He also wears a crown of skulls and a tiger skin. His body is circled by a necklace of skulls, his face contorted with fury. He brandishes a thunderbolt sceptre, and tramples underfoot forces inimical to the Dharma.

Lastly we come face to face with Dorje Drolo ('immutable guru with loose-hanging stomach'). He rides through the jungle of life on a tigress. His expression is ferocious, and he is enhaloed with flames. His massive dark brown body is garlanded with skulls. He waves a thunderbolt in his right hand, and points a phurba with his left, to ward off all threatening forces. This is Padmasambhava as subduer of demons.

These are eight of the forms that Padmasambhava assumes. They could be said to represent the guru's resourcefulness in transforming his approach to each situation, so as to teach in an appropriate way. He is not fixed in any mode of being or acting. Knowing that his nature is as empty as the blue sky, he can shift shape spiritually and psychologically, like clouds sculpting themselves into different forms and then dissolving. For stubborn-minded enemies of the Dharma, the guru musters even more power and energy; for those open to the sūtras he teaches sūtras; for those ready for the mysteries of Tantra he demonstrates Tantra. In this way he exemplifies *upāya*, or skilful means – the flexibility of the Buddhist teacher.

Padmasambhava's eight forms could also be seen as the same principle at work on different levels of consciousness. To the rational mind the guru appears as a pandit or a Buddha, and proclaims teachings on the Four Noble Truths and so forth. However, deeper more primitive strata of the mind are not amenable to being taught in this way. These aboriginal levels of consciousness need to be converted through the magic powers of figures like Nyima Odzer and Dorje Drolo.

In summary, we can say that these differing manifestations mark Padmasambhava as the embodiment of all the resourcefulness of Buddhist teaching. They show him as the typical Tantric guru – working through logic and reasoning to convert the rational mind, but also diving deep into the psychic depths to confront, subdue, and transform the powerful and primitive – perhaps even demonic – energies that inhabit those dark realms.

Though we have looked at so many forms, we have yet to meet Padmasambhava in his most frequent manifestation, as a king of Zahor. In a sense you most truly meet a vajraguru when you receive initiation from him. So we shall try to venture out into the unknown to meet the Precious Guru, and be empowered with his knowledge, power, and compassion. We shall ask him to grant us *siddhi*, both mundane powers and the supreme *siddhi* of Enlightenment. These powers are emphasized in Padmasambhava's mantra: *oṃ āḥ hūṃ vajraguru padma siddhi hūṃ*.

To meet him we have to go to the place of initiation, to enter his secret realm. His realm, in which he flies like a great eagle, is the blue sky of śūnyatā. Initiation can only take place if we let drop our barriers and habitual ways of being, forsake our own territory, and enter the state of spiritual openness.

In the vast blue sky appears a fiery-red lotus. On the lotus is a red sun disc (symbol of compassionate skilful means) lying horizontal; on the sun disc a white moon mat (symbol of the wisdom of realizing Emptiness). We wait, expectant. The lotus throne and sun and moon mats are like a great stage, on which the hero of a cosmic drama will appear. The blue sky above the moon mat begins to glow with brilliant light. The radiance gradually takes form, until we see a blissful young man seated before us. (This is how he usually appears, though sometimes he can manifest instantaneously, from a dazzling bolt of lightning.)

He is dressed in robes.[28] The outermost is a beautifully decorated red cloak. This symbolizes the Mahāyāna. It is outermost because it is love and compassion which the Precious Guru offers to the world in all situations. Beneath the red cloak he wears the yellow robes of a monk – showing that though he follows the Tantric path beyond conceptual distinctions of right and wrong, he keeps pure his ethical discipline. He has not abandoned the basics of Buddhism, but simply carried them up into a higher vision. Beneath these he wears a blue robe. Blue was the royal colour in ancient India. It became associated with the Tantra, as it incorporated much of the symbolism of royalty into its ritual. For example, we have seen that the Tantric initiation procedure in which the initiate is sprinkled with water from an initiation vase by the guru parallels the ceremony of anointing a king. So the blue robe which Padmasambhava wears, most hidden and closest to his heart, symbolizes the Vajrayāna.

He wears Tibetan-style boots, and sits totally relaxed, his left foot tucked up, his right resting at a loose angle. His right hand rests on his right knee, holding the vajra of Truth itself. He clasps it with his middle fingers, while his index and little fingers are outstretched, in the mudrā of warding off demons and enemies of the Dharma. It is said that Padmasambhava's power increases as worldly conditions deteriorate. He is the supreme alchemist, the master who transforms hatred into wisdom, craving into love, darkness into light. The more powerful the forces of evil become, the more lustrous his form appears. In the depths of despair and annihilation, his diamond wisdom shines like a great lamp. Difficulties, opposition, and danger fuel his spiritual power.

In his left hand he holds a skull cup filled with something that looks suspiciously like blood. The skull cup represents śūnyatā, and the liquid it contains is the amrit-nectar of Great Bliss.

With the realization of the emptiness of self and others, a revolution takes place in our experience. The forces of desire, which caused us so much restlessness and pain, now give us bliss. The problem with pleasure is that we usually experience it within the framework of subject and object. It reinforces our feeling of being an 'I', 'in here', trying to incorporate a pleasurable stimulus 'out there'. The result is craving and frustration. When self and other dissolve away, there is just enjoyment, with no attempt to nail it down, or strangle it by repetition. William Blake well sums up the difference:

> He who binds to himself a Joy
> Doth the wingéd life destroy;
> But he who kisses the Joy as it flies
> Lives in Eternity's sunrise.[29]

The skull cup symbolizes the death of the ego, the spiritual death which creates space – the experience of the 'open dimension' of śūnyatā. The nectar is like blood, for blood is life, the free-flowing energy capable of assuming any form , which is released with Insight. In Nyingma circles this ambrosia – the Great Bliss experience – is often symbolized, for obvious reasons, by beer or wine. Rising up out of the skull cup is a vase of the Nectar of Immortality. Above it is a precious jewel – the wish-fulfilling gem of the Bodhicitta.

In the crook of Padmasambhava's left arm nestles a trident staff, known as a *khaṭvāṅga*. It is adorned with a number of strange objects. A *damaru* hangs from it. There are crossed vajras. Above them is a vase of initiation adorned with victory pennants. Then there are three human heads: one freshly severed, one decomposing, the top one just a skull. Finally, the staff is surmounted by a flaming trident.

The net of symbolic associations surrounding the different elements of the staff is complex, and we do not have space to discuss them individually. We shall look at just two aspects of the staff overall. The first is that the staff is spoken of as the hidden consort. According to the biography of Yeshe Tsogyal, who was one of Padmasambhava's chief female disciples, at one point the Precious Guru wanted to travel with her, without her being seen, so he magically transformed her into his staff.[30] Thus the khaṭvāṅga symbolizes all the spiritual qualities that the Vajrayāna associates with the feminine (principal among which is wisdom). Padmasambhava's holding the staff indicates that he has perfectly integrated these qualities.

Also, the khaṭvāṅga is a magic staff, and Padmasambhava is the peerless spiritual magician. It was through his magic powers that he defeated the Bon shamans and subdued the demons of Tibet. Through his sādhana you magically transform yourself, turning the base metal of your mundane consciousness, the lead of ignorance, into the gold and jewels of Tantric attainment.

On his head the Precious Guru wears a lotus cap – red in colour. It is one of many hundreds of kinds of hat to be found in the Tantra – each with its own particular significance. This one has flaps which can come down over the ears. On its front are five jewels, arranged in a mandala pattern – white in the centre, blue, yellow, red, and green around – symbolizing the five wisdoms. Above them is a crescent moon surmounted by a golden sun. These symbolize the subtle energies of the psychophysical organism, which Padmasambhava has unified, thereby bringing an end to all dualistic thoughts. The cap is crowned with a half vajra with a vulture's feather rising out of it. The vulture is a bird associated with yogins – because it is said to be the bird that flies the highest.

Padmasambhava wears ornate earrings, and a priceless necklace of jewels. He has long flowing locks, a moustache, and a small pointed beard. His gaze is piercing. His face has a strange expression, a kind of compassionate smile, but tinged with wrathfulness. His smile is a challenge. We can say that it symbolizes the union of compassion (the smile) and wisdom (the wrathful gaze), but that does not explain it away. This wrathful smile is a key to understanding Padmasambhava. It is mysterious and unfathomable. Sometimes when his visualization dissolves I am left with the after-image of that dangerous smile, hanging in the sky like an Enlightened version of the Cheshire Cat. But, if Padmasambhava is a cat at all, he is a leopard or tiger of the Dharma.

His body is adorned with what are called his three vajras: a white *oṃ* at his forehead, a fiery red *āḥ* at his throat, and a deep-blue *hūṃ* at his heart. They are like three special concentrations of Padmasambhava's immense spiritual power. It is from them that, if one is ready to run the gauntlet of the blue sky and dare that dangerous smile, one will receive the Precious Guru's initiation, be empowered with both mundane *siddhis* and the supreme *siddhi* of Enlightenment itself, and become a king or queen of the Dharma.

The Kagyu lineage

Within any school of Tibetan Buddhism there will be many lineages of teaching. Here we shall concentrate on the lineage which is of central importance to the Kagyu school. It is quite commonly represented in Tibetan *thangkas*. This lineage does not begin with any historical person, but with Vajradhara – the Buddha who embodies the primordially awakened mind, and to whom many Tantric teachings are attributed. He sits cross-legged on a multicoloured lotus, his body deep blue in colour, and adorned with silks and jewels. In his right hand he holds a golden vajra (his name means 'vajra holder'), in his left a bell with a vajra handle.

For me, the most striking aspect of this Buddha is the mudrā he is making. His hands are crossed in front of his heart, so that the inside of his right wrist touches the outside of his left wrist. The mudrā suggests in a particularly striking way the union of opposites. Right crosses over into left, and vice versa. Wisdom and compassion meet, and become inseparable. The vajra and vajra handle of the bell incline toward one another, suggesting the crossed vajra, symbol of totality, of Amoghasiddhi.

After Vajradhara in this chain of Tantric transmission comes Tilopa (988–1069). He received Tantric teaching directly from Vajradhara in visions. He is one of the group of eighty-four *mahāsiddhas* – teachers who gained great spiritual accomplishment and supernormal powers over the world of appearances through Tantric meditation. Like most of the *mahāsiddhas* he is usually portrayed seated on an antelope skin – a symbol of the Bodhisattva's vow never to abandon suffering beings. He wears just a loincloth and a meditation sash (a cord used to help maintain the body upright during long periods of meditation). Indian by birth, he is brown-skinned and has long black hair hanging loosely over his shoulders. In some representations he is shown with a skull cup and a damaru. In others he holds a fish. This is a reminder of his meeting with his disciple Nāropa.

Nāropa (1016–1100) was one of the greatest scholars of his day. He lived at Nālandā, the great Indian Buddhist university, where he was renowned for his ability to triumph over non-Buddhists in debate. (As the terms of the debate were often that the loser together with all his followers should convert to the winner's faith, this was a very useful skill!) However, one day, while he was studying, Nāropa had an encounter with a strange old woman, who seemed to have appeared out of nowhere.[31] She made him see that while he knew a tremendous amount about the Dharma, and could expound and debate it, he had not made it his own. It was all just book knowledge. Seeing this, Nāropa had the courage to leave Nālandā and all the acclaim he received there.

He wandered alone in search of Tilopa, who, he believed, could show him the Tantric path of direct experience. The account of his wanderings is like a dream story or hallucinatory vision. All the situations he encountered were clouded by his own dualistic views. Eventually he came to a house where he had been told Tilopa was staying. Upon entering, he saw a fierce, dark-skinned man frying live fish over a fire. This, of course, was completely antithetical to the compassion which Nāropa, as a 'good Buddhist', expected of Tilopa. He was scandalized. However, he was considerably more shocked when Tilopa snapped his fingers and the fish returned, unharmed, to their lake.

This story is typical of the *siddhas*. Their life stories are full of symbolic teachings and demonstrations of supernormal powers developed through Tantric practice. They live in a world beyond all opposites, and far beyond social conventions.

Nāropa stayed with Tilopa for twelve years, giving himself completely to his service. He would do anything Tilopa asked, even if it was likely to entail suffering or risk of death. Finally Nāropa came to understand the Dharma, not just with his head but with his heart, even with his bones. Nāropa is usually depicted in very similar fashion to Tilopa, but holding a skull cup and vajra-bell or other Tantric emblems. In some *thangkas* he is blowing a ram's horn.

One of Nāropa's chief disciples was Marpa (1012–96), who made the arduous journey across the Himalayas from Tibet to the plains of India three times. He brought back many teachings, including the famous six yogas of Nāropa, which he translated into Tibetan. By the time of his third visit he himself was a teaching. He was not a monk or a renunciant. He maintained a farm, and had a wife and children. Tantric life stories interweave fact and symbolism. Marpa's wife's name is Dakmema – which is the Tibetan for *nairatmya*, which means 'empty of self nature'. At her death she is said to have dissolved into Marpa's heart.[32]

Marpa is usually depicted as stocky, with long black hair, dressed in the clothes of a Tibetan layman. He sits in meditation posture, with his hands resting on his knees, palms downward.

Next in the lineage we come to Milarepa (1052–1135), probably Tibet's most famous spiritual figure. Milarepa's early life was a disaster. Through practising black magic he destroyed many people. Once converted to the Dharma, he realized that he would need a very potent method of practice to counterbalance the unskilful karma he had piled up, and put himself in Marpa's hands. Marpa refused to grant him Tantric initiation and gave him backbreaking work instead. So hard and irascible was Marpa that Milarepa several times came close to despair. Finally, Marpa explained that he had treated Milarepa in such a way to help him purify the karma of his earlier evil life. Then he lovingly gave him initiation.

Milarepa spent the rest of his days meditating in the remote wilderness areas of Tibet, often high up in the Himalayas. He became a master of *tummo*, the practice of psychic integration, whose by-product is increased bodily heat. Adepts in this practice are known as *repas* (cotton-clad ones)

Milarepa

because they wear only a single cotton cloth, even when living in caves above the snow line.

In later life Milarepa continued wandering from place to place meditating. In addition, he began teaching, and gathered many disciples around him. He had the capacity to sing spontaneous songs illustrating any aspect of the Dharma. These songs, sung a thousand years ago in the caves and villages of one of the most inaccessible countries on Earth, are still echoing around the world, and providing inspiration for a new generation of Buddhists in the West.[33]

Milarepa is usually depicted seated in a cave, wearing his white cotton garment. He has long black hair. Sometimes his complexion has a greenish tinge – a reminder of his austerities: for long periods he meditated alone in the mountains, living on nettles. He holds his right hand to his ear, as though listening to an inner voice of the Dharma. According to some authorities, though, this is a yogic posture, designed to affect the body's subtle energy flow.

Milarepa had many great disciples, but for the Kagyu lineage one is especially important. Gampopa, or Dakpo Lharje (1079–1153), was trained as a physician. On the death of his wife he devoted himself to the Dharma, making intensive study of the Kadampa teachings. He subsequently met Milarepa, and became one of his 'heart sons'. He it was who formed the line of practice brought to Tibet by Marpa into a distinct school of Tibetan Buddhism. He also wrote a renowned text known as *The Jewel Ornament of Liberation*.[34]

Gampopa is normally portrayed in monastic robes, wearing the red hat characteristic of his school. One of Gampopa's chief disciples was Dusum Khyenpa (1110–93), the first Karmapa, who founded the Karma Kagyu sub-sect, which has been very active in establishing Dharma centres in the West.

Looking at this lineage one is struck by how differences of lifestyle made little or no difference to these men. So often in religious traditions a split will develop between an ecclesiastical hierarchy and a mystical tradition, which is viewed with suspicion by the hierarchy as a possible breeding-ground for heresy. The Kagyu lineage flows smoothly from a yogin to a scholar turned yogin, thence to a lay farmer, on to a cotton-clad ascetic, then to a monk and writer. Such a lineage, unruffled by matters of outward appearance, must have a strong hold on the inner reality which gives birth to all forms of life.

The five masters of the Sakyapas

The word *sakya* means grey earth, and refers to an area of hillside of an unusual colour on the banks of the Trom River in Tibet which was the site of the founding of the first monastery of the Sakya order in 1073 by Khon Khonchok Gyalpo, a member of the powerful Khon family. He had studied with the great Tibetan translator Drokmi (992–1072). Drokmi was a holder of a set of teachings known as Lam Dre (path and fruit) which centre on the meditational practice of Hevajra, one of the yidams of Highest Tantra whom we shall meet in the next chapter. These Lam Dre teachings are the central focus of Sakya spiritual practice.

The lineage of the Lam Dre stems from the great Indian *mahāsiddha* Virūpa (or Birwapa). He was a monk who became abbot of the Buddhist university of Nālandā. Devoting himself to Tantric practice, he spent many long years meditating single-pointedly on the Highest Tantra yidam Cakrasaṃvara without achieving any result whatsoever. Finally, in despair, he threw his mālā – the beads on which he had counted millions of seemingly fruitless mantras – into a cesspit and decided to give up his meditation. That night, in a dream, he was approached by Nairātmyā, the Tantric consort of the yidam Hevajra. She told him to go and recover his mālā and wash it with perfume. He did as she instructed, and she initiated him into the mandala of Hevajra. She appeared to him again on the following nights, and soon he had gained total confidence in the Tantric teachings from his own direct experience. Having experienced the absolute truth, he no longer felt bound by social conventions. He left Nālandā singing, and then travelled from place to place teaching and helping people through the extraordinary powers he had obtained through Tantric meditation.

Virūpa appeared in a vision to Khonchok Gyalpo's son, Sachen Kunga Nyingpo (1092–1158), who was the first of the 'five masters' or 'five great ones' of the Sakyapas. Kunga Nyingpo had received the entire Lam

Dre teaching from his guru, but after an attack of food poisoning he found he had forgotten the instructions. As these special teachings were only passed on orally, and there was no one with whom he had direct contact who could repeat them to him, his situation was very difficult. In response to this crisis he meditated one-pointedly, invoking his guru, and was rewarded with a vision of Virūpa, surrounded by four of his disciples, his dark brown body shining like a hundred thousand suns. Virūpa gave him the complete teaching. Applying himself to meditation on Hevajra, Kunga Nyingpo came to equal the great Indian Tantric masters in his spiritual realization.

The second of the five masters was Kunga Nyingpo's son, Sonam Tsemo (1142–1182), who did much work in systematizing the Tantric literature. He was directly inspired by Avalokiteśvara. The third of the five is his younger brother Drakpa Gyaltsen (1147–1216), a renowned scholar and yogin, who is said to have been continuously helped by the Bodhisattva Mañjuśrī.

Sakya Pandita (1182–1251), grandson of Kunga Nyingpo, is the fourth of these great gurus. He is considered an emanation of Mañjuśrī. He was responsible for the full assimilation into Tibet of the system of logical analysis of the Indian master Dharmakīrti, and in general the range of his studies and writings mark him as one of the greatest of all Tibetan Buddhist scholars. In addition to this, he was recognized as one of the greatest teachers of his generation by Godan Khan, the Mongol emperor, who invited him to his court. In Mongolia he caused Buddhist practice to become widespread. It is said that after his death he was reborn in the Pure Land of Akṣobhya where he gained complete Enlightenment.

The close relationship built up by Sakya Pandita with the Mongol emperors was cemented by his nephew, Chogyal Phakpa (1235–1280), the last of the five masters. He conferred Hevajra initiation on Godan Khan's successor, Kublai Khan. In response, the emperor appointed Phakpa imperial preceptor – which was tantamount to being secular ruler – of Tibet. As a result, the Tibetans were ruled from the monastery at 'the place of grey earth' for nearly a century.

In Tibetan Buddhist art these Sakyapa gurus are depicted in various ways. Sometimes Sakya Pandita may be the central figure with the rest of the five masters ranged around him. He is usually depicted holding the stems of two lotuses on which rest a flaming sword and a book, symbolic of his being an emanation of Mañjuśrī, and wearing monastic robes and a red cap. Alternatively Kunga Nyingpo may be the central figure, flanked by Drakpa Gyaltsen and Sonam Tsemo (forming a group traditionally known as the Three White Ones), with Sakya Pandita and Phakpa (the Two Red Ones) below them. In such pictures Virūpa will often be shown near the top of the picture, portrayed as an Indian yogin, seated on an antelope skin and pointing to the sky. This commemorates an episode in which he is said to have stopped the sun in its tracks through his yogic powers. The story is almost identical to the one we encountered earlier about Padmasambhava. Virūpa plunged his phurba into the earth at the place where light and shade met, stopped the sun, and drank an alehouse dry.[35]

Je Tsongkhapa

The main guru visualized by the Geluk ('virtuous ones') or Yellow Hat school, is their founder, Je Tsongkhapa. He was born in Amdo, a province of eastern Tibet, at sunrise on 21 November 1357, in an area known as Tsong-kha (region of onions). It is from this place that he takes the name by which he is generally known, though his religious name was Lozang Drakpa, and he is often referred to as Je Rimpoche ('great lord of religion') by Gelukpas.

He entered a monastery at a very young age, where he mostly studied the Kadam teachings – the school founded by the Indian teacher Atīśa, who had come to Tibet in the eleventh century and made many reforms. However, Tsongkhapa also studied with teachers of other schools, such as the Kagyu. (He wrote a commentary on the six yogas of Nāropa.) From the age of sixteen he studied the five traditional monastic subjects: logic, Perfection of Wisdom, Madhyamaka philosophy, *abhidharma*, and *vinaya* (monastic discipline), and mastered them in the exceptionally short period of seven years.

After studying under forty-five different masters representing all the main traditions, he founded Ganden monastery in 1409, where he established the Geluk order (although at first his followers took their name from the monastery and were known as the Gandenpas). The Geluk school places particular importance upon monastic discipline. It also stresses intellectual clarity about the Dharma – derived from study and debate – as a foundation for contemplative practice.

Throughout his life Tsongkhapa had many visions of Mañjuśrī, and with his aid came to a profound understanding of the Madhyamaka interpretation of the Perfection of Wisdom. Indeed, Tsongkhapa was an original thinker in this area, so that from him the Geluk school has a distinctive philosophical position on śūnyatā. He wrote extensively on both sūtra and Tantra, and made Atīśa's teaching of the Lam Rim (graduated path)[36] the structure on which he based his teaching. The Lam Rim lays out the stages of the path from suffering and helplessness to Supreme Enlightenment in a clear, systematic way. Reading Lam Rim texts we are shown clearly how step by step we can transform ourselves, and how this process will eventually enable us to arrive at Buddhahood. It also demonstrates the need for a firm basis in the practice of the other two *yānas* before one can practise advanced Tantric teachings. Tsongkhapa wrote three great texts on the Lam Rim. It is these Lam Rim teachings – most fully expounded in his Lam Rim Chenmo – which form the basis for most of the teaching of Gelukpa lamas in the West – usually via a commentary on Tsongkhapa's work by the renowned Phabongka Rimpoche (1878–1941).

His Geluk school spread quickly, and he attracted many disciples. His two chief disciples were Khedrup Je and Gyaltshap Je. They are often shown flanking Tsongkhapa in *thangkas*. (Khedrup Je is usually to our right as we look. He can be distinguished by his bulging eyes and more wrathful expression.) They are sometimes depicted as part of a group of eight, known as the eight pure disciples, who were specially chosen by Tsongkhapa to go into meditation retreats with him. Gyaltshap and Khedrup Je became in turn the first holders of the title of 'throneholder of Ganden' (Tibetan *Ganden Tripa*). It is the Ganden Tripa, not the Dalai

Lama, who is the head of the Geluk order. The post is usually held for seven years.

One of Tsongkhapa's disciples, who came to study with him four years before he died in 1419, was a man called Gedundrup, who was retrospectively recognized as the first Dalai Lama. The line of Dalai Lamas, seen as emanations of Avalokiteśvara, continues down to Tenzin Gyatso, the fourteenth Dalai Lama, who is now a world figure, spreading the Buddhist message of peace and compassion, despite having been driven into exile by the Chinese. The fifth Dalai Lama united Tibet under one secular leadership, becoming both spiritual and temporal leader of Tibet. He was also responsible for building the Potala Palace in Lhasa as we know it. (Work began in 1645, and it was not completed until thirteen years after he died. Amazingly, news of his death was kept secret until the building was finished.) Many of the Dalai Lamas are portrayed in Tibetan religious paintings, but pictures of the Great Fifth, as he is known, are by far the most common.

Having learned a little of Tsongkhapa's life, and seen the decisive influence he had on Tibet (the Gelukpas are the majority school among Tibetan Buddhists), it is time we met him face to face. Here we shall draw on a description of part of a visualization written by the fourth Panchen Lama, Tenbay Nyima, early in the nineteenth century.

We have to allow everything to dissolve away into that Emptiness which, with Mañjuśrī's help, Tsongkhapa understood so deeply and explained so incisively. Out of that infinite space appear eight great lions. Their magical appearance in space does not negate their essential voidness. Their voidness of self-nature does not prevent their appearance. We can see every hair of their manes, can see their teeth as they throw back their heads, and yet they are like illusions created by a conjuror, or apparitions in a dream.

The lions support a magnificent throne, on which sits Tsongkhapa on a lotus, with mats of sun and moon. He is wearing the three yellow robes of a monk. His face is a clear white, smiling serenely. On his head is a golden pandit's hat. He is seated in the full-lotus posture, in the middle of a five-coloured aura. He is making the mudrā of turning the Wheel of the Dharma. His hands hold the stems of lotuses, which open out into blue blossoms, one at each shoulder. For the rest of the visualization we shall quote the Panchen Lama's text:

> Upon the blossoming blue lotus at his right shoulder, the wisdom of all the Buddhas is embodied in the form of a flaming sword. Its light fills the world, and the flame that burns from its tip consumes all ignorance. Upon the blossoming blue lotus at his left shoulder is a volume of the *One Hundred Thousand Verse Prajñāpāramitā Sūtra*, the sole mother of all buddhas of the three times. On its sapphire pages are glowing letters of burnished gold, from which shine rays of light, clearing away the ignorance of living beings. These letters are not just shapes, but speak out in a clear tone the stages, path, and final goal. They proclaim the way of acting for the benefit of all living beings, beginning from the first arising of bodhi-mind to the twenty-seven great deeds of a buddha. Merely by holding this image in mind, you are awakening the inclination to the Mahāyāna path.
>
> Seated in the heart of Tsongkhapa is the Conqueror Śākyamuni, and seated in his heart is the Conqueror Vajradhara. In each pore of Tsongkhapa's body are countless buddha-fields, and from each of these, innumerable rays of light shine in the ten directions. On the tip of each ray appear an inconceivable number of buddhas, equal to the number of beings in saṃsāra. The actions of each buddha are for the benefit of all living beings.[37]

Tsongkhapa's emblems, the sword and the book, show that he is believed to be an emanation of Mañjuśrī. As we contemplate his figure, we can absorb something of his wisdom by reciting his mantra: *oṃ āḥ guru vajradhara sumatī kīrti siddhi hūṃ*. *Sumatī kīrti* means 'famed for your beautiful mind'. Now, five-and-a-half centuries after his death, Tsongkhapa's fame is being carried round the world by the many Gelukpa lamas teaching in the West.

Vajrabhairava

Five

The Oath-Bound Deities

If you move in Tibetan Buddhist circles, it will not be long before you hear someone talk about their yidam. Especially if they have been meditating for some years, you will gather from the way they talk that it is something of the greatest importance for them. This Tibetan word literally means oath, vow, or promise, and connotes the Buddhist deity to whose meditation you are committed, to whom you are linked by a promise or vow, your main focus of spiritual practice.

Any Buddhist deity can be a yidam. For example, many of the early Kadampa geshes had Tārā or Avalokiteśvara as theirs. However, the word is sometimes reserved for deities of the *anuttarayoga*, or Highest Tantra. Initiations into this level of practice require great seriousness on the part of the initiate. When receiving them, one takes various vows and pledges. Some initiations may include a commitment to practise the sādhana every day for life. In this way the initiate is 'bound by oath' to the yidam. In this chapter we shall use the word to refer to the deities of Highest Tantra.

These yidams are all embodiments of Tantric teachings, in the same way that the goddess Prajñāpāramitā came to embody the Perfection of Wisdom literature. Each of them has a Tantric text, or collection of texts, of whose teachings they are the living symbols. None of them, to the best of my knowledge, is found in the Mahāyāna sūtras.

As always with the profusion of forms in the Tantra, there are a great number of these yidams. Here we shall look at just five of the most important, and try to gain a feeling for them as a class.[38] In particular we shall concentrate on the yidams Cakrasaṃvara and Vajrabhairava, as representatives of the two main divisions of Highest Tantra. The tantras of this level can be divided into Mother Tantras, which are primarily concerned with the development of wisdom (Sanskrit *prajñā*), and Father Tantras, which emphasize the development of compassionate skilful means (Sanskrit *upāya*).

We shall only be able to gain a general feeling for these five yidams – firstly because they are the most complex figures in the whole of Buddhism (both iconographically and in the world-view which they embody). Secondly, some aspects of their practice are genuinely secret, and it would be inappropriate for me to offer too many details about their inner meaning and the way they are meditated upon. Writers on Highest Tantra have to try to tread a 'middle way'. On the one hand, details of these practices are not supposed to be revealed to those who have not received the relevant initiation. On the other, there has been a general relaxation of secrecy by Tibetan teachers, and it would be ridiculous to ignore the fact that much information has already been published in the West. However, I feel it is wise to err on the side of caution, and I have thought it best to give something of an outsider's view of these figures, even where I might have some personal experience. I have also decided against providing any of the mantras associated with them.

The view of existence which the yidams express is more multifaceted than that of other figures. Broadly speaking, we can say that each Buddha or Bodhisattva embodies a particular approach to Enlightenment. For example, the Green Tārā practitioner strives to develop infinite compassion, Vajrapāṇi's is a path of liberating energy, and so on. The yidams, however, are more multidimensional. Rather than one approach to the universe, they present an all-encompassing vision of it. They are complex symbols that have many levels of interpretation, outer, inner, and secret. At the diamond gates of their mandala, we enter a cosmic labyrinth of multiple meanings in which truths echo and re-echo forever.

This vision is made more total because, unlike the majority of practices of the Lower Tantras, one aims to keep the meditation going all the time. After the Green Tārā sādhana, when we rise from our cushion, the meditation has had its effect, but we return largely to our old self. Practice of Highest Tantra aims to cut off the old self altogether. At initiation we become the yidam, and we aim to live as the yidam from then on. After finishing the sādhana we get up still trying to maintain the feeling that we are the yidam, that everything we hear is the mantra, and that our environment is our mandala palace and attendant deities. Through transforming ordinary appearances and concepts in this way, we aim to superimpose our meditative vision on every aspect of our lives, to transform them totally.

The complex and radical nature of these practices is reflected in the yidams' iconography. Here we move away from a more naturalistic vision to one in which we may encounter twin figures, with perhaps twelve, sixteen, or thirty-four arms. According to Chögyam Trungpa, many of these forms are based on those of yakṣas – powerful spirits of ancient Indian legend – who appear in the sūtras. Generally, though, they bear a close resemblance to the Shiva figures of Hinduism.

Many of the figures are recognizably human in physique, though some are heavily built. Many are neither peaceful nor wrathful, but somewhere in between – smiling, but also sneering. This semi-wrathful expression suggests a balanced attitude to the world, as though the yidams fuse in themselves the natures of both the peaceful and wrathful Buddhist deities.

The yidam is also known as the 'esoteric' Dharma Refuge. While some of these practices may be genuinely secret, the word 'esoteric' here also suggests something that is a matter of personal experience. The yidams become hardly less esoteric by being unveiled in the West in exhibitions and coffee-table picture books on Tibetan Buddhism. It is only when we enter their mandala, and actually see for ourselves their total vision of the universe with its interplay of energies, that their secrets will be revealed.

Why should the yidam be a Dharma Refuge? We have seen that the term 'yidam' can be applied to any Buddhist figure who is the main focus of our meditation and devotion. Let us suppose that the beautiful young female bodhisattva Green Tārā is our yidam. We may spend quite a bit of time reading and studying the Dharma, but if for an hour a day, say, we become Tārā, in a world of light in which we see the sufferings of sentient beings before us, and play out the drama of rescuing them, and in which everything ends by dissolving into the sky of Emptiness, that is the experience likely to leave the deepest imprint on our minds. It is contact with the yidam through meditation that will give us the strongest taste, the most direct experience, of the Dharma. It is through our Tārā meditation that we take the Dharma into our heart and make it our own. Hence the yidam is the esoteric Dharma Refuge.

Heruka Cakrasaṃvara

The tradition of meditating on this yidam is based on the Śrī Cakrasaṃvara Tantra. This tantra has been widely studied by all Tibetan schools, and there are many sādhanas and commentaries associated with Cakrasaṃvara. He is a yidam of particular importance to the Kagyu school, though as with all the yidams we shall be meeting, devotion to him crosses all sectarian frontiers. His practice is very widespread among the Gelukpas. There is a sādhana known as the 'Yoga of the Three Purifications of Śrī Cakrasaṃvara' that is quite widely practised at Gelukpa centres in the West.

The first in the line of Cakrasaṃvara practitioners is generally considered to have been the Indian *mahāsiddha* Saraha. He was a brahmin who had become a Buddhist scholar-monk. However, he was not satisfied by his learning, and set out to find a Tantric teacher. In a market-place he saw a young low-caste woman making arrows. He became deeply engrossed in watching her working, and finally approached her and asked if she made arrows for a living. She replied, 'My dear young man, the Buddha's meaning can be known through symbols and actions, not through words and books.' Her arrow hit its mark. Flouting all convention, Saraha went to live with her, receiving her Tantric teachings. As a result, he became one of the greatest of all Tantric adepts. He is particularly renowned for his *dohas* or songs, in which he expresses the profound realizations he has gained through Tantric practice.

This yidam is known by various names in Sanskrit. Sometimes he is known as Saṃvara or Śambara, sometimes as Heruka. In Tibetan he is called Khorlo Demchok or Khorlo Dompa. Here we shall refer to him as

Cakrasaṃvara. Though it literally means 'restraint', *saṃvara* is associated, by Tibetan lamas explaining the significance of this yidam, with 'supreme bliss'.[39] *Cakra* (now usually anglicized as chakra) means wheel. It is also the Sanskrit word used for the psychic centres within the body of the meditator, whose manipulation through performing the Cakrasaṃvara sādhana gives rise to the 'supreme bliss'.

As we have seen, texts of Highest Tantra are often classified into Mother and Father Tantras. Mother Tantras emphasize wisdom – particularly the realization of the indivisibility of bliss and Emptiness. They are particularly suited to those of passionate temperament, providing methods of liberating the energy tied up in greed and attachment and making it available for the pursuit of Enlightenment. Cakrasaṃvara is a central deity of the Mother Tantra class. He can appear in a number of different forms. Here we shall describe just one very well known and characteristic form.

He appears standing on a variegated lotus. Even in this small detail, we see how this world of Highest Tantra differs from the world of the Mahāyāna occupied by the Buddhas and Bodhisattvas, most of whom were symbolized by one predominant colour. In the world of the yidams we are gazing at an all-encompassing vision, so colours become more varied.

He stands on a sun disc, on which lie two figures being trampled underfoot. One foot pins down the black god Bhairava by the back of the neck, the other is placed on the breast of the red goddess Kālarātri. Both figures have four arms, two of which hold a curved knife and a skull cup, while the other two are raised in devotion to the great figures above them.[40] Bhairava and Kālarātri are forms of the god and goddess Shiva and Uma. Shiva is one of the most powerful of all Hindu deities. In later Hinduism he forms one of a triad of gods with Brahma and Vishnu, and is responsible for all the destructive aspects of the universe. Uma is his consort. In the Vajrayāna they are incorporated into the Tantric world-view as minor deities who preside over the desire realm. They are symbolically overcome by Cakrasaṃvara, and raise their hands in submission to the transcendental figures that stand over them. Even the highest forms of the mundane appear puny compared to the majesty of this yidam.

His body is deep blue, and he has four faces which gaze out into the four cardinal directions. The face that looks directly at us is blue, the one to our right, green, to our left, yellow, and facing away from us, red. All the faces have crowns of skulls. In his hair, to his left, is a crescent moon.

This moon, along with many of the other emblems of Cakrasaṃvara, is an attribute of Shiva.[41] All these Shivaite symbols are given a strictly Buddhist interpretation in the Vajrayāna. Here, for instance, the crescent moon symbolizes Bodhicitta which is ever-increasing. Thus the general suggestion of the figure is of an Enlightened consciousness, having overcome and gone beyond the relatively limited vision represented by Shiva, nonetheless expressing itself through the symbols associated with him. The power of such an image is likely to be largely lost on Westerners. One would perhaps have to imagine Cakrasaṃvara trampling underfoot the prostrate form of the God of the Old Testament to gain some idea of its potency in India.

Cakrasaṃvara has a tiger-skin draped over his loins, and a garland of freshly-severed heads hangs from his neck. He has no less than twelve arms. A central pair embrace his consort Vajravārāhī ('diamond sow'). The two hands cross behind her back, holding a vajra and bell in the *vajrahuṃkāra* mudrā. The right hand with the vajra, and the left with the bell, cross at the wrist, the right arm outermost. His other arms radiate out from his body, forming a rough circle. The right hands, beginning from the top, hold (1) an elephant hide, which is draped across his back, (2) a damaru, (3) an axe, (4) a chopper with a vajra handle, and (5) a trident lance. His left hands, counting downwards, hold (1) the elephant hide, (2) a khaṭvāṅga, or magic staff (similar to the one we saw Padmasambhava holding), (3) a skull cup brimming with nectar, (4) a noose or lasso, and (5) the severed head of the god Brahma, which has four faces.

He is locked in sexual embrace with his consort Vajravārāhī, who by contrast is quite a simple figure. She is brilliant red, with only one face and two arms. Her right hand, raised aloft, holds either a vajra or a flaying-knife (Tibetan *drigu*) with a vajra handle. Her left hand, embracing her partner's neck, holds a skull cup. She is naked apart from a few bone ornaments, a five-skulled crown, and a garland of skulls which hangs from her neck. In some forms both her legs are wrapped around her partner's thighs, in others her right leg is raised while with her left leg she also tramples on Kālarātri. The copulating figures are encircled by an aura of flames.

The symbolism of these figures is so complex, so labyrinthine, that a guru experienced in the Cakrasaṃvara system could easily produce a large book on just this one figure. The most important message it conveys is a logic-bemusing union of opposites. Heruka Cakrasaṃvara and his consort appear from the dimension in which all diversity is unified, and unity displays its endless forms.

The two figures on which the mystic pair drum their feet lie separate. They represent the realm of mundane experience in which separation is the rule. It is this separation, experienced by most people as isolation, which fuels desire. Desire urges us to unite, to reach out to overcome separation. But this external seeking gives us at best only temporary relief for our ills. Eventually we lie separate and alone, in the world of me and you, he and she, good and bad, heaven and hell. Constantly discriminating, reaching out to embrace some experiences and avoiding others, we fail to see that the two parts of all dualities are attached; we cannot grasp one without finding ourselves holding on to the other.

Cakrasaṃvara and his consort unite all opposites in their sexual embrace. They are really one figure, appearing as two. Their union represents different integrated aspects of one Enlightened consciousness. They exemplify what in Tantra is called *yuganaddha* – 'two-in-oneness'.[42]

We saw in Chapter One that the female figure, the *yum* or Mother, is also referred to as the *prajñā* – for she represents wisdom, the intuitive realization of Emptiness. This wisdom sees the common characteristic of all phenomena: everything is devoid of an unchanging, fixed, self-nature. Everything has the same essential nature, which is 'no-nature'. This wisdom-view applies to everything in the universe. Because nothing has a fixed nature of its own, there are no fixed boundaries or divisions between things. If there are no fixed limits or barriers, if the seemingly static elements of existence can recombine like the colours of oil on water, then there is no separation. Everything is of one empty nature. Hence the *yum* has only one face, symbolizing this essential sameness of all things. She is naked to symbolize the simplicity and unadorned nature of things in their essence. (In Mother Tantras the female consort is always naked, whereas in Father Tantras the consort always wears some item of clothing – usually just a cloth around the loins. This indicates that Mother Tantra is mainly concerned with the wisdom that sees the essential emptiness of all forms; Father Tantra emphasizes the compassionate expression of wisdom through form.)

In contradistinction to her, the male *yab*, or Father, represents the compassionate activity of the Enlightened mind – working in the world to awaken beings to their true empty nature. In fact, with his four faces looking into the four directions, and his twelve arms, he symbolizes the world of appearances, the multiplicity of forms. His partner is the unchanging realization of the emptiness of appearances, the sameness of nature of all forms. Their sexual union suggests the ultimate non-distinction, on the level of absolute truth, between appearances and Emptiness. Their being two figures suggests that distinctions can still be made on the level of relative truth.

The twelve arms of the male figure represent correct understanding of the twelve links of conditioned co-production (*pratītya samutpāda*). This basic Buddhist teaching is an application of the principle that all things come into existence dependent on particular conditions, and cease to exist when those conditions change. It applies this general principle to demonstrate the conditions that cause our existence in the circle of saṃsāra, the endless round of unsatisfactory rebirth. These are essentially ignorance of the true nature of existence, which causes us to react to pleasant and unpleasant stimuli with desire or aversion. This strengthens our involvement with these stimuli, which fixes our view of them and embroils us more deeply in the world of impermanence and hence unsatisfactoriness.

In each hand he holds an implement which symbolizes the overcoming of saṃsāra. For example, the elephant hide he holds draped over his back is said to symbolize conquered ignorance, the axe severs the fetters of birth and death, and so on.

Thus the two figures represent a vision of a new universe, which we can enter through contemplating them. In this universe, opposites are united without losing their distinct validity on the relative level. Dwelling on Cakrasaṃvara we gain direct intuitive experience of the highest teachings of the Dharma. The opposites of appearances and emptiness, diversity and unity, saṃsāra and nirvāṇa, compassion and wisdom, discrimination and sameness, relative and absolute, male and female, all fuse in the two ecstatic figures, and this fusion of opposites causes the dawning of great bliss in the mind of the meditator, a bliss of which sexual union can be only an inadequate cipher.

There are still more opposites that we can find reconciled in this mystic coupling. Wrathfulness and peacefulness are reconciled. It is said of the male figure that while outwardly fierce, he is inwardly compassionate, dignified, and serene.

More important, we find symbols within symbols. On the level of the overall figures, the male Heruka symbolizes skilful means, while his partner stands for wisdom. However, the *yab* holds in his front two hands the crossed vajra and bell, which themselves represent conjoined method and wisdom. Again, in the pairing of figures, the *yum* is receptive, the male active and outgoing. Yet we see that both these attributes are to be found in the female figure alone. Her left arm and side are passive, and in her left hand she holds the skull cup. Yet her right side is dynamic. With her right leg (in some traditions) she grasps her partner's thigh, and her right hand is thrust upward brandishing aloft the sharp vajra-chopper, or the dynamic vajra, with her hand in the *tarjanī* mudrā of warding off demons. From this we can see that yet another pair of opposites has fused: macrocosm and microcosm have become one, and the great truths of the Dharma can be seen in the vast and the infinitesimal.

We still have a further step to go before we can grasp even the rudiments of the Cakrasaṃvara universe. The great *yab-yum* pair are but the central focus of a vast mandala. There are a number of important Cakrasaṃvara traditions, passed down from Indian masters, with mandalas involving different numbers of figures. A common form has sixty-two deities, but some mandalas include several hundred figures altogether. For example, a mandala in the tradition of Maitrīpada has twelve ḍākinīs, four in an inner circle, and a further eight in an outer ring, of whom four have animal heads and guard the gates of the mandala. All the ḍākinīs are naked like Vajravārāhī. They each have four arms, and these hold a knife, skull drum, skull cup, and trident staff.

To begin to describe a sādhana of Cakrasaṃvara would take more space than we have available, since the visualizations of yidams of Highest Tantra tend to be long and complex. Anyway, as I have said, of all visualizations these are the ones least put on display to the general public. I hope our meeting with Cakrasaṃvara has been long enough to give us some feeling for him, and for us to begin to see why these yidams should be the esoteric Dharma Refuge. A Tantric practitioner in retreat might spend many hours a day in repeated performance of a Cakrasaṃvara sādhana. Through recreating him- or herself out of Emptiness in the form of Cakrasaṃvara united with Vajravārāhī, he or she enacts a cosmic drama of the true nature of phenomena. With repeated practice, even when not formally meditating, he or she experiences the ordinary world of appearances as a mandala in which all opposites are transcended but not obliterated, and dwells in the blissfulness of the two-in-oneness of unity and diversity which is just one of the messages of Cakrasaṃvara.

Vajrabhairava

Vajrabhairava (Tibetan *Dorje Jikje*) can be translated 'diamond terror (or terrifier)' or 'terrifying thunderbolt'. Unlike the rest of the yidams described in this chapter, who are semi-wrathful, Vajrabhairava appears in a very powerful and wrathful form indeed. As such he might well appear in Chapter Seven, when we encounter the wrathful deities and protectors of the Dharma. However, he functions as a yidam, or high patron deity. Indeed, he is one of the most commonly invoked.

He is one particular form of a deity called Yamāntaka (Tibetan *Shinjeshe*). This means Slayer of Death. Yamāntaka is the wrathful form of the peaceful Bodhisattva of Wisdom, Mañjuśrī. One Tibetan legend delivers an account of how he acquired his name. A yogin was once meditating in seclusion in a mountain cave. He was on the brink of Enlightenment when some robbers who had stolen a yak entered his cave, lit a fire, and started to cook it. The yogin was lost in contemplation, and it took them some time to notice his silent figure. Fearing that he would act as witness to their theft, they killed him by cutting off his head, thus denying him the prize of Enlightenment in this life, which had come so close. In fury, the yogin used magic power to attach the yak's head to his headless trunk. He then killed the robbers and stormed through the land slaying everyone he met.

So terrified were the people of this rampaging murderer that they invoked Mañjuśrī, who took the form of Yamāntaka, and slew this yak-headed Death. Thus he became known as Slayer of Death. Obviously the name can have a much less literal meaning than that of the story. The Enlightened mind slays death by liberating itself from any necessity to take enforced rebirth in saṃsāra. (We shall not enquire too closely into how a yogin who was really on the verge of Enlightenment could have reacted with such murderous fury at being interrupted....)

Several texts of Highest Tantra are associated with Yamāntaka. He is a member of the so-called Vajra family of Akṣobhya, and is particularly concerned with overcoming the poison of hatred. His meditation belongs to the Father Tantras. These are considered to be particularly appropriate for those of a wrathful temperament. They include various means of using energy which is characteristically expressed as anger in order to further spiritual progress. In its advanced stages it is particularly concerned with the development of a subtle bodily form known as the illusory body (Sanskrit *māyākāya*, Tibetan *gyulu*).[43]

There are several forms of Yamāntaka, including a red one, but usually he is a deep blue-black. Different Tibetan schools tend to invoke different forms. The Karma Kagyus are devoted to the Black Master of Life. A form favoured by the Nyingmapas is Quicksilver, a poison-faced, dwarf-like figure, whose lower body is a magic dagger. There is also a yellow form which is included among a very important set of Nyingma figures known as the eight Herukas (Tibetan *Kagye kyi lha tshok*). However, the most commonly encountered form is Vajrabhairava. This figure is particularly invoked by the Gelukpas, and occupies a quite central place in their monastic practice.

Vajrabhairava is a powerful, massive, deep-blue figure, enhaloed – as always – with the flames of wisdom knowledge, which burn up all obscurations. He has nine heads, looking in different directions. These symbolize the nine divisions of the Buddhist scriptures. The main head is that of a buffalo, his two great horns representing the Two Truths and the paths of method (or skilful means) and wisdom. The head which surmounts all the others is that of the Bodhisattva Mañjuśrī. (At times it can be comforting to look at his golden face, to reassure ourselves that the menacing Vajrabhairava is really 'on our side'.)

He is sometimes meditated upon in union with his consort, Vetālī ('vampire lady'), who is also blue in colour. However, he is also quite frequently visualized without a consort in a form known as Ekavīra, meaning solitary hero.

He has thirty-four arms, nearly all bearing different weapons and other implements. In his right hands he wields a curved knife, a dart with three peacock feathers, a pestle, a fish knife, a harpoon, an axe, a spear, an arrow, an iron hook, a skull-topped club, a khaṭvāṅga, a wheel of sharp weapons, a vajra, a hammer, a sword, a hand-drum, and an elephant hide. His left hands hold a skull cup, a head of Brahma with four faces, a shield, a leg, a noose, a bow, intestines, a vajra-bell, a hand, a scrap of cloth from a graveyard, a man impaled on a stake, a triangular brazier, a scalp, an empty hand making a threatening gesture, a trident with a banner, a fan, and another part of the elephant hide. The order of the implements occasionally varies.

All these implements have their own symbolic value, with meanings traditionally assigned to them, that can be overlaid with one's own personal associations. There is no space here to examine all of them. To take just one example, the fan is used to waft the flames when performing a fire puja – a tantric ritual involving making burnt offerings – and is traditionally said to represent the illusory (Sanskrit *māyā*) nature of all things. But this implement for stirring the air is also associated in my mind with a Zen story.[44] One day, two monks had an argument about a fluttering flag. One said the flag was moving. The other said it was really the wind that was moving. Their master Hui Neng, the great sixth patriarch of Zen, happened to be passing and overheard the dispute. He gave his verdict: 'It is neither the wind nor the flag which is moving. It is the mind.' So this one emblem, held in the sixteenth of Vajrabhairava's left hands, could in itself become quite a rich subject for meditation. One could never completely explore all the associations that the total figure conjures up.

Vajrabhairava has sixteen legs, eight trampling to his right, eight stretched out to his left. Under his feet lie all kinds of animals: a dog, a sheep, a fox, and so on. These figures can be seen as enemies of the Dharma that he has subdued, or, more psychologically, aspects of the meditator's lower nature whose energies have been harnessed and pressed into the service of the spiritual quest. With symbolism there are no 'right answers'. For example, Tsongkhapa states that the sixteen crushed creatures stand for the eight abilities and the eight surpassing forces. When interpreting symbolism it is never a question of 'who is right?' As Saint Augustine said of the Bible, 'The more interpretations the better.'[45]

Hevajra

The tradition of meditation on the yidam Hevajra (Tibetan *Kyedorje* or *Gyepa Dorje*) stems from the great king of Uḍḍiyāna, Indrabhūti. From him it was passed down through a chain of Indian Tantric practitioners including Mahāpadmavajra, Anaṅgavajra, and Saroruha, and found its way to Tibet in the eleventh century.

The Hevajra Tantra, of which the yidam Hevajra is the personification and embodiment, is a tantra of the Mother class.[46] It has been very influential on the whole field of Tantric practice. (It is in the system of Hevajra that the very important yoga known as *tummo*, the psychic heat yoga, first appears.) The word *he* is a joyful exclamation, meaning something like 'oh!' *Vajra*, of course, is the diamond thunderbolt. According to David Snellgrove the name is 'derived from the salutation "*He Vajra*" ("Hail Vajra!"), with which a master acclaims his pupil after the relevant consecration.'[47] Sometimes Tantric exegesis associates *he* with compassion, and *vajra* with wisdom.

Hevajra is the most important yidam for the Sakya school of Tibetan Buddhism, but once again his practice traverses sectarian boundaries.

For example, Marpa, the teacher of Milarepa and forefather of the Kagyu school, was a very adept practitioner of the Hevajra methods. Indeed, reading the description of his household in the life of Milarepa, one gains the impression that Marpa's farm was a symbolic mandala of Hevajra. As we saw, his wife was even called Dakmema, which is the Tibetan for Nairātmyā, the name of Hevajra's consort.

It is this interweaving of levels: the physical with the spiritual, the everyday with the symbolic, that is the hallmark of Tantra. We have seen that *tantra* means something woven, and that it is the Tantric initiate's aim to interweave all opposites, including the warp of the mundane and the weft of the transcendental, until everything, on every level, is redolent of one non-dual Reality.

Hevajra is a wrathful emanation of the Buddha Akṣobhya. He is usually depicted dancing, in the position known in Sanskrit as *ardha pariyaṅka*. As with all these yidams, he has several forms. He has manifestations with two, four, six, or sixteen arms. Once again we shall look at the most complex figure, as it gives the best feeling for the yidam's unique characteristics. There are two sixteen-armed forms, both deep blue. One, known as Kapāladhara Hevajra, holds skull cups; the other, Śastradhara Hevajra, bears mostly weapons. We shall look at the former.

Kapāladhara Hevajra has eight faces, the central one is blue. Each face has three eyes, and is semi-wrathful in expression. He wears a necklace of skulls, and embraces his consort Nairātmyā ('empty of a self'), who is also blue in colour.[48] He has four legs, and is dancing on four figures who lie on a sun disc atop a lotus throne. The four figures symbolize the four Māras or demons who embody all the active hindering forces – within the psyche and in the objective world – that work to deflect us from the spiritual goal.

Hevajra's sixteen arms spread out in an arc, eight on each side, each holding a skull cup. In the skull cups in his right hands are a white elephant, a green horse, an ass with a white blaze, a yellow ox, a grey camel, a red man, a blue stag,[49] and a black cat. In his eight left hands the skull cups contain symbols of earth, water, fire, air, moon, sun, Yama (lord of death), and Vaiśravaṇa (lord of wealth). These symbols represent the eight *lokapālas* (guardians of the world) and the eight planets.[50] There is no room to explore them here. Hevajra's is a complex system of practice that was traditionally taken up only after years of study and preparation.

Like all the yidams, Hevajra stands in a magical dwelling in the centre of a great mandala. He and his consort are surrounded by eight more female figures in the eight directions. Each is of a different colour and holds a different emblem. For example, in the south-west is the blue Caṇḍālī ('fiery one') holding a wheel in her right hand and a plough in her left. These eight figures with their colours and emblems add yet more layers of meaning to the multidimensional universe in which the Hevajra practitioner aims to take up permanent residence.

Guhyasamāja

Guhyasamāja (Tibetan *Sangwadupa*, sometimes abbreviated to *Sangdu*) means Secret Assembly. The full title of the Guhyasamāja Tantra literally means 'the secret union of the body, speech, and mind of all the Tathāgatas'. This tantra is concerned to produce an experience of Enlightened consciousness that is without beginning or end, whose nature is the union of wisdom and luminosity.

The Guhyasamāja Tantra was one of the earliest to be committed to writing. Tradition has it that King Indrabhūti of Uḍḍiyāna saw some monks, whose spiritual realization had given them supernormal powers, flying in the air over his lands. He wanted to emulate them, but insisted that he would need a method of meditation suitable for those who had not renounced sense-pleasures. In response, Śākyamuni taught him the Guhyasamāja Tantra.[51] By following this practice the king and all the people of Uḍḍiyāna attained Tantric realization.

The teaching was then conveyed to another king in southern India called Viṣukalpa, who taught it to Saraha, the *mahāsiddha* whose name is also associated with Cakrasaṃvara, who then gave it to Nāgārjuna. It was then preserved orally, until written down by Asaṅga. It entered Tibet during the early spread of Buddhism there, and a number of Nyingma lamas wrote commentaries on it. It was retranslated in the eleventh century by the Tibetan monk Rinchen Zangpo (958–1055), known as the Great Translator.

The Guhyasamāja Tantra has had a profound effect on Tantric Buddhism. In its first chapter, the *adi-* (or primordial) Buddha – i.e. absolute Reality beyond time and space – gives birth, through the power of mantric sound, to the entire mandala of the five Buddhas with their consorts. (In this case, Akṣobhya (imperturbable) inhabits the centre of the mandala, and Vairocana (illuminator) sits in the east.)

There are two main schools of Guhyasamāja practice: the Ārya school, whose central teacher was Nāgārjuna, and the school derived from Jñānapada. In the Guhyasamāja system, any one of several deities can be the central figure of the mandala. In the Jñānapada school it is Avalokiteśvara. In the Ārya school, two main mandalas are meditated upon. In one the central figure is Mañjuvajra, a form of Vajrasattva.[52] However, the most important figure in the main mandala of the Ārya school, is Akṣobhyavajra. It is this figure that is often just described as Guhyasamāja in books and catalogues of Tibetan *thangkas* and images, and it clearly relates to chapter I of the Tantra. It is a beautiful deep-blue, seated form, in sexual embrace with the light-blue consort Sparśavajrā. Both *yab* and *yum* are smiling (though the mother is said to be very fierce), and decked with silks and jewels. They each have three faces: blue, red, and white. Their blue principal faces are close to each other, with the others on either side. They represent the transmutation of passion, aggression, and ignorance into expressions of wisdom. Each face is adorned with a third, wisdom eye in the forehead. The *yab* sits in the vajra posture,[53] with the *yum* in his lap, her legs encircling his waist in sexual embrace.

The figures have six arms. The *yab* embraces the *yum* with his principal arms, his crossed hands holding a vajra and bell, as we saw with Cakrasaṃvara. At the same time, the *yum* embraces the *yab* with two of her arms, also holding a vajra and bell. In his other right hands the *yab* holds the wheel and the lotus. In her other right hands, on the opposite side of the figure, the *yum* holds the same emblems. In their other left hands both *yab* and *yum* hold a jewel and a sword.

Those familiar with the five Buddhas of the mandala will recognize their emblems: Vairocana's wheel, Amitābha's lotus, Ratnasambhava's jewel, and Amoghasiddhi's sword (though his emblem is more commonly the double vajra). In the Guhyasamāja system, Akṣobhya occupies the centre of the mandala, so the figure's central hands hold his emblem the vajra, and the vajra-bell.

This figure, once one has accustomed oneself to the strangeness of the multiple heads and arms, becomes one of the most beautiful of all Buddhist images. It is a symbol of a psyche, and a universe, in which everything is in perfect harmony. The faces are serene, the sitting posture has a calmer feel than the dancing and trampling of the other yidams we have met. *Yab* and *yum* perfectly mirror each another in their hand positions and emblems. They, and all the opposites they represent, are in total accord.

Even the two sides of the figures are in balance. Drawing a vertical line through the centre of the figures would still leave two harmonious sides with all the six emblems. We are in a world where opposites attain a two-in-oneness, and the same cosmic laws can be demonstrated in the macrocosm or microcosm.

The Father and his consort are seated in the middle of a mandala palace surrounded by thirty other deities. Once again we have symbolism of the connectedness of macrocosm and microcosm, for the retinue of the central pair, who themselves hold the emblems of the five Buddhas, includes Vairocana, Ratnasambhava, Amitābha, Amoghasiddhi, and their consorts.

Guhyasamāja is a particularly important yidam for the Gelukpas. Their two main Tantric colleges, the Gyuto and Gyume, which used to be based in Lhasa, both gave great prominence to the practice of his sādhana, and the Guhyasamāja system is used by the Gelukpas as the paradigm for approaching an understanding of other Highest Tantra systems of practice.

Guhyasamāja belongs to the Vajra family of Akṣobhya. His practice belongs to the Father Tantra, which concentrates on compassion and skilful means, using complex yogic methods to bring about the development of the illusory body. Father Tantra, as we have seen, is concerned with the transmutation of anger and aggression. The Guhyasamāja Tantra is basically concerned with the realization that the universe is inherently wondrous and valuable. This can only come about when the passions, in particular hatred and aversion, have been transmuted.

Kālacakra

Kālacakra is a yidam who has become quite well known in Tibetan Buddhist circles in the West. This is because a number of lamas have given mass initiations into his practice. The Dalai Lama has given Kālacakra initiations attended by thousands of people in a number of places in Europe and America, as well as in India.[54] In consequence, several books on the Kālacakra system are now available in the West.

This practice of giving mass initiation for a yidam of Highest Tantra is very uncommon, and gives Kālacakra a peculiar significance for the Tantric tradition. In a way, the initiation is regarded as more general, and the commitments one takes are not seen as being as serious as those for other Highest Tantra initiations. The Tibetans consider that, while of course one should make every effort to take the initiation and the commitments seriously, the act of simply attending and participating will be beneficial. The initiation will plant seeds of a positive nature in one's mind which, if tended, can ripen at a later date as catalysts of spiritual progress. These initiations then take on the significance of large festive occasions, auspicious for all those who attend them in good faith.

Kālacakra (Tibetan *Du Kyi Khorlo*, sometimes abbreviated to *Dukhor*) means 'wheel of time', and time is one of the central concerns of the Kālacakra system. Especially in the commentaries on this tantra there is a great deal of discussion of time and transcending time – as the experience of Enlightenment transcends time and space. In general, this system of Tantric practice uses a developed view of time to arrive at the Timeless. It is usually classified as a Mother Tantra, and both deity and tantra are highly regarded by all Tibetan schools. It is an exceedingly complex system of thought and practice, which has outer, inner, and secret levels. The outer teachings of Kālacakra are concerned with astronomy, astrology, and mathematics. The inner teachings deal with the body and its energy channels. The secret teachings are the actual instructions for meditating on the Kālacakra mandala.

Plate One Heruka Cakrasaṃvara

Plate Two Vajrabhairava

Plate Three Kālacakra

Plate Four Vajravārāhī

Plate Five Vajrayoginī in a form also known as Sarvabuddhaḍākinī

Plate Six Six-Armed Mahākāla

Plate Seven Śrīdevī

Plate Eight Śākyamuni Refuge Assembly from the Gelukpa tradition

According to tradition, the Kālacakra Tantra was proclaimed by the Buddha, himself appearing in the form of Kālacakra a year after his Enlightenment.[55] He taught the Tantra at Dhānyakaṭaka in southern India, inside a huge stupa, at the request of King Sucandra. Sucandra was king of Shambhala – a legendary country to the north-east of India. The king returned to Shambhala, built a three-dimensional mandala of Kālacakra, and made Tantric Buddhism based on the Kālacakra system the state religion.

The Kālacakra teachings were propagated in Shambala by a line of kings. The eighth, Mañjuśrīkīrti, initiated many people into the Tantra, and also composed a short text – the 'Condensed Kālacakra Tantra' – which is what is now generally known as *the* Kālacakra Tantra. In consequence he became known as Kulika (one who bears the lineage). According to tradition, the Kālacakra teachings are still being propagated in Shambala by the Kulika kings. An Indian master from Orissa called Cilupā is said to have travelled to Shambala and returned with Kālacakra teachings, which were subsequently passed on to Nāropa and then to Atīśa. The fact that there is no trace of the Tantra in India before Cilupā has led some scholars to suggest that the Tantra originated somewhere in central Asia.

The Kālacakra teachings came to Tibet with Atīśa in 1026. Their introduction into Tibet led to a new system of measuring time in sixty-year periods. Five elements, fire, earth, water, wood, and metal, were added to the twelve-year system by which each year is attributed to one of the signs of the zodiac.

The Kālacakra system was studied by all schools of Tibetan Buddhism. It was propagated by the great Sakyapa lamas Sakya Pandita and Phakpa. Tsongkhapa, the founder of the Geluk order, wrote several short works on it, and his two main disciples both wrote extensive commentaries.

To achieve a clear visualization of the most complex mandala of Kālacakra would be a meditative *tour de force*. One would have to become, in meditation, a four-faced male deity with consort, standing on the figures of Kāmadeva (the Indian god of love) and Rudra. Two goddesses, the consorts of the subjugated gods, hold on to Kālacakra's heels, their heads bowed.

The *yab* is blue, and has six shoulders, twelve upper arms, and twenty-four lower arms. The lower arms are arranged in three sets of four on each side, each set of a different colour. The uppermost set on each side is white, the middle red, the lower blue. Each of his arms holds a symbolic implement, such as a sword, a wheel, or an axe. Even his fingers are of different colours.

As Kālacakra one would embrace the consort Viśvamāṭa (mother of all). She is yellow in colour, with four faces and eight arms. She holds a curved knife, an iron hook, a damaru, and a rosary in her right hands, and a skull, a noose, a white lotus, and a jewel in her left. One would see oneself standing in the middle of a glorious palace at the centre of a five-levelled mandala-palace, surrounded by a radiating pattern of hundreds of figures.[56]

The yidam and his mandala fuse time and the Timeless, the 'endless round' and absolute Reality, into one non-dual vision in which neither polarity is suppressed. Perhaps one day we shall see Western tantras produced which combine our knowledge of astronomy and other sciences with the profound Enlightened viewpoint of the Buddha. What extraordinary figures, what marvellous mandalas, could such a vision produce!

Ḍākinī visualized in the Chöd rite

Six

Dancing in the Sky

In the last two chapters we have met the guru and the yidam, the esoteric versions of the Buddha and Dharma Refuges. Now it is time to meet the ḍākinī, the third esoteric Refuge, the hidden jewel – the hidden ruby, we could say – of the Sangha.

Personally, I think it is impossible to produce an adequate definition of a ḍākinī. To attempt to catch a ḍākinī in the iron trap of mundane logic is a hopeless task. In one Sanskrit dictionary the word *ḍākinī* is said to refer to a class of flesh-eating demoness. The Tibetan translation, *khandroma*, means female sky-goer. Sometimes she is referred to as a sky-dancer. The male counterparts, *ḍākas*, do exist, but they play a relatively insignificant role in the Tantra, whereas ḍākinīs are central to it.[57]

Rather than define the ḍākinī, let us try to see the situations in which she appears. We have seen that she is the esoteric Sangha Refuge, so we can expect her to be related to the guru in the same way that the Sangha is related to the Buddha. The Sangha is the community of all those who are learning from the Buddha how to follow the path to Enlightenment. The Sangha gathers round the Buddha as often as possible – to learn from him and for the sheer pleasure of being with him. On the esoteric level, then, we should expect to find ḍākinīs clustering around the vajraguru.

This is indeed the case. If you find the vajraguru, the ḍākinīs will not be far away. However, the Tantric guru – the 'thunderbolt guru' who will stop at nothing to show you Reality – is often difficult to find. For example, Nāropa spent a very long time searching for Tilopa. When you do find the guru he will often be in a strange or frightening place: on an island in the middle of a poisonous lake like Kukkurīpa (one of Marpa's gurus), in the depths of the jungle like Nāropa, or most frequently in a cremation ground. It is in places like these that you find the vajraguru, and so it is in these fearsome places that you will meet the ḍākinīs. Padmasambhava, for example, spent many years meditating in cremation grounds (that had names like Piled-Up Corpses, and Sleep in the Mysterious Paths of Beatitude). In each one he feasted and danced with the ḍākinīs, and taught them the Dharma.

So to meet a ḍākinī is not easy. They are not domesticated but wild. To find them you have to leave behind the security of your views and ideas. You have to abandon the tidy civilized world of mundane concepts. You have to walk out into the unknown, the unexplored, the unimaginable.

A Tibetan yogin named Khyungpo Naljor visited India many times, searching for a highly-realized teacher who could show him the way to full Enlightenment. All the teachers he met told him that he should try to meet the yogini Niguma, who had been the disciple and Tantric consort of Nāropa. On simply hearing the name of Niguma, Khyungpo Naljor was filled with great happiness, and he set off to find her. He had been told that she had gone beyond any dependence on the physical body, but that she sometimes appeared in a certain cemetery.

When he arrived in the cemetery, the yogin fearlessly sat himself down in the midst of the corpses and the wild animals that dwelt there. As a result, he had a vision of a brown ḍākinī. She was completely naked, except for a few ornaments, all made of human bone. She had a khaṭvāṅga and carried a skull cup. She was dancing ecstatically in the sky high above his head. At times she multiplied herself into many wild dancing figures, filling the sky, at others there was just one great figure in the air above him.

Khyungpo Naljor realized he must be in the presence of Niguma, and asked for instruction. But the ḍākinī said that she was an ogress, and when her helpers arrived they would feast on his blood; he had better escape while he still had his skin. Kyungpo Naljor ignored this threat, and continued asking for teaching. Seeing that he could not be scared away, the ḍākinī changed tack. She asked him for a large amount of gold for her teaching. (In Tantra it is usual to give something of value for initiation, to demonstrate one's seriousness, and out of gratitude for the immense spiritual riches to which the empowerment gives access.) Kyungpo Naljor had saved up a great deal of gold with which to seek teachings in India. Very reverently he offered it all to the ḍākinī. Without a moment's hesitation she threw it away into the jungle.

If there had been any doubt in the yogin's mind before, it was wiped away by this evidence of the ḍākinī's complete non-attachment, even to tremendous wealth. He knew that he was dealing with an Enlightened teacher. The ḍākinī then proceeded to give him initiation, much of it in dreams.

In this story we see how the ḍākinī can appear. She irrupts out of another realm. It can happen anywhere, at any time, but she reveals herself most truly when she dances free in the sky of Emptiness. There is nothing fixed about her, though. She is quite capable of shifting shape. She may manifest as a beautiful young maiden or goddess, or as a decrepit old crone. The ḍākinī Vajrayoginī appeared to Nāropa as a hag with thirty-seven ugly features. (After she had convinced Nāropa to seek Tilopa, and then vanished like a rainbow, Nāropa sang a song giving thirty-seven similes for the dangerous and unsatisfactory nature of saṃsāra.)

The ḍākinī may appear as voluptuous and alluring, or as threatening. (Niguma first warned Kyungpo Naljor that she was a flesh-eating demoness.) Some ḍākinīs are part animal. They may have the heads of boars, tigers, crows, bears, jackals, or a host of other strange creatures. Their bodies can be any of, or all of, the colours of the rainbow. Most usually, however, the ḍākinī appears as a naked, dishevelled, dancing, witch-like woman. Her element is the sky, and it is there that she dances.

Let us look more closely at one of the most important of all ḍākinīs. This is Vajrayoginī (Tibetan *Dorje Naljorma*), who to Nāropa appeared withered and wrinkled (perhaps because he had lost himself in scholarship, so the upsurging forces of inspiration, which ḍākinīs embody, had become dull and neglected.) More commonly, Vajrayoginī appears as a sixteen-year-old girl, an age considered by Indians to be the prime of youth. She is a virgin, symbol of her complete innocence in relation to saṃsāra. Her body is a brilliant, fascinating red – the colour of arousal and passion, for Vajrayoginī is fiercely in love with the Dharma. She has flowing dishevelled black hair, for she has gone beyond concern for worldly appearances. She dances, abandoning herself to the inspiration of the Dharma.

In her right hand she brandishes a vajra-chopper above her head. This is a brutal implement, used by butchers for cutting and flaying. It has a vajra handle, and its blade is razor-sharp. With her chopper the ḍākinī cuts off all attachment, especially concern for the physical body. For the faint-hearted, the brandished vajra-chopper is a threat of destruction. For the brave it is an invitation to approach and be cut free of all limitations. In her left hand she clasps to her heart the skull cup of śūnyatā, filled with the ambrosia of Great Bliss, for it is this *mahāsukha* which the ḍākinī pours out like wine to her devotees.

On her head is a tiara, for she is spiritually rich. However, rather than jewels, it is set with five human skulls. These are reminders of the Wisdoms of the five Buddhas in a form that cannot be ignored.

Around her neck hangs a garland, not of flowers but of human heads, freshly-severed and dripping with blood. There are fifty of them. These correspond to the sixteen vowels and thirty-four consonants of the Sanskrit alphabet, known as *āli* and *kāli*. As her ornaments they symbolize that the ḍākinī has purified speech on the subtlest level. The circle of heads also suggests the endless round of birth and death. The ḍākinī thrusts herself beyond it, and life and death become her ornaments. Thus she wears armlets, wristlets, and anklets of human bone. In the centre of her chest, secured by strings of bone, is a mirror in which all beings can see the effects of their past actions. These adornments are the ḍākinī equivalents of silks and jewels – symbolizing the six Perfections of the Bodhisattva. While ḍākinīs are beautiful and can appear in wondrous raiment, it is as though they are too close to the realities of existence to cover themselves in pretty, alluring things. They are the Truth, and you can take them or leave them, they are not going to try to entice you. It is as though the Bodhisattvas such as Avalokiteśvara and Tārā are the Dharma experienced in the warmth of the heart. Ḍākinīs are the Dharma felt in one's guts.

In the crook of her left arm Vajrayoginī holds a magic staff, similar to Padmasambhava's. This symbolizes her mystic consort. Though she appears in female form, the ḍākinī is not lacking in masculine qualities. She is the perfect synthesis – feminine and masculine dancing together. The masculine is present, but more hidden and inward.

She dances with her right foot raised, so that her legs form a rough bow and arrow shape. The supporting left leg is the bow, the upraised right the arrow. The bow and arrow are important symbols in Tantra, symbolizing the inseparability of wisdom and method. With her left foot she is trampling on a prostrate human figure – symbol of the craving, hatred, and ignorance that she has subdued, and which she now victoriously stamps into the ground. Yet she is not concerned with what is happening under her feet. Her mastery of saṃsāra is so total that she flattens obstacles effortlessly, like a small boy treading on an ant.

The whole movement of her being is upwards. Her hair stands on end. She leaps as she dances, as though impatient to take off into a higher dimension. In the centre of her forehead is a third eye, for she is able to see a higher truth, a wisdom beyond duality. All around her body, flames leap upwards. These are the fires of her soaring inspiration, her unquenchable energy, her purifying wisdom. They are fires of love burning for all that lives.

Her expression is ecstatic. She is drunk with wisdom, entranced with spiritual power, wild with compassion, insatiable for truth. At the same time her look is dangerous, warning. Like all ḍākinīs, she doesn't fool around.

The more frequently visualized ḍākinis

The Tantra recognizes three orders of ḍākinī, the lowest of which have not emancipated themselves from saṃsāra and may be either helpful or hostile to human beings. The middle order is associated with twenty-four sacred places to be found in India and Tibet, and can only be perceived by those who are spiritually developed. These twenty-four sites are also related to aspects of the subtle body, and in some forms of advanced Tantric practice ḍākinīs of this order are visualized within one's body. The highest order is known as 'spontaneously Enlightened' and consists of emanations of the *dharmakāya*. Most of the ḍākinīs we shall look at in this section belong to this highest order, being embodiments of full Enlightenment.

We have already met Vajrayoginī in one of her principal manifestations. She can be red or white, though red is more common. As we shall see, though ḍākinīs can be of any colour they are frequently red, as they are associated with passion and intensity in the quest for Enlightenment, and the fiery upsurging forces of spiritual inspiration.

Vajrayoginī is visualized in many different forms of Tantric practice. For instance, in a Nyingma sādhana of Guru Yoga one transforms oneself into Vajrayoginī. Above one's head is one's own teacher, and above him, one above another in the sky, is the lineage of gurus, going back through time to its Enlightened source. One becomes Vajrayoginī in this practice to emphasize receptivity to the gurus of the lineage, and perhaps to attract their blessings magically, by appearing in the most fascinating form possible.

Vajrayoginī is also a central figure in the *tummo* or 'heat yoga', which is the first of the 'six doctrines' of Nāropa and Niguma. This advanced practice is capable of increasing bodily warmth, rendering one impervious to cold. Though much is made of this by some Western writers, it is really only a side-effect. The main purpose of the practice is to produce an extraordinary concentration of psychophysical energy. This is done by inducing the subtle energies of the body to become unified by entering the central channel of the subtle energy pathways within the body. Inducing these energies to enter the central channel produces a very strong experience of blissfulness. As we saw in Chapter One, combining this blissful experience with contemplation of śūnyatā is an extremely effective way of gaining full realization. Vajrayoginī is visualized in the *tummo* yoga, as she symbolizes particularly the union of Emptiness and Great Bliss. Her red colour also suggests the blazing fire of *tummo*.

Another appearance of Vajrayoginī occurs in the Chöd Rite, which we shall examine briefly when we meet Machik Labdron. In general, Vajrayoginī appears in many Tantric practices, as well as having a number of sādhanas of Highest Tantra devoted purely to her.

Vajrayoginī appears in several forms other than her dancing one. For instance, she can have the same colours, implements, and so on, but be stepping to the left, with her right leg outstretched. In this form, she is also known as Sarvabuddhaḍākinī (ḍākinī of all the Buddhas), for she is that huge wave of passionate commitment to Truth and Freedom which has carried all the Buddhas to Enlightenment. In Tibetan, this form is known as Naro Khacho – the ḍākinī of Nāropa. Her practice is one of the thirteen 'golden dharmas' of the Sakya school of Tibetan Buddhism. This time both her feet stamp on samsaric figures. In this position she no longer waves the chopper aloft; it is held loosely by her right side, as though it has done its work. Here she perhaps emphasizes the stage of the path beyond that at which one needs to cut down the promptings of saṃsāra. If you have to cut them down, you are still involved with them, still using energy in fighting them. Beyond this you reach a relaxed state in which the mind can be left alone. Your understanding of Reality is such that thoughts and emotions can be allowed to form themselves and dissolve away, like bubbles on a stream.

If her right hand has relaxed, her left now comes fully into play. The skull cup is no longer held to her heart but aloft, above her head, which is tilted back, as she quaffs a flow of the red light-nectar of Great Bliss, which looks just like blood. Blood is life, and the ḍākinī drinks incessantly, becoming filled with spiritual zest and energy. Her large breasts are thrust forward, symbolizing her capacity to bestow Great Bliss on all beings.

Another almost identical form of this ḍākinī, which is of particular importance for the Kagyu school of Tibetan Buddhism, is Vajravārāhī (Tibetan *Dorje Phamo*). She can only be distinguished from the dancing form of Vajrayoginī by one characteristic. In her piled-up hair appears the head of a sow. Vajravārāhī means diamond sow. The pig or sow is a Buddhist symbol for ignorance. It appears at the centre of the *bhavacakra*, or Wheel of Life, in a kind of dance with the snake of hatred and the cock of craving. The three career round in a circle, each one biting the tail of the one in front. The sow in Vajravārāhī's hair is like a trophy. She has severed the head of the sow of ignorance with her vajra-chopper, and brought the drunken dance of saṃsāra to an end.

Machik Labdron

Similar again is Kurukullā (Tibetan *Rikjema*). Another red, dancing figure, she is holding not a vajra-chopper and skull cup but a flowery bow and arrow. These are the weapons of Kāmadeva, the Indian god of love – half-brother to Cupid, and just as good a shot. Kurukullā's function is to fascinate people. By a kind of love-magic she leads even enemies of the Dharma to fall at her feet. Sometimes she has four arms, so that as well as the bow and arrow she holds a hook and a noose. Having shot her victims, she pulls them in with the hook and binds them with the noose. Some of her Tantric rituals are not for the squeamish, and perhaps come a little close to black magic.[58]

Perhaps the most extraordinary of all these red ḍākinī forms is one described in the *Sādhanamālā*, and associated with the tradition of Śavaripā. Here, she stands in an aggressive stance, holding the vajra-chopper in her right hand and her own head, which she has severed, in her left. She is flanked by the ḍākinīs Vajravairocanī and Vajravārṇanī. Three streams of blood spurt from her headless neck and flow into her own mouth and the mouths of the two other ḍākinīs. The severing of the head symbolizes the cutting off of all ego discrimination.

We have seen that not all ḍākinīs are emanations of Emptiness. There are a number of great female Tantric teachers who achieved the 'status' of ḍākinīs, and are often represented in dancing ḍākinī form. We have already met Niguma, the disciple and Tantric consort of Nāropa, who became a great teacher in her own right, and started an important lineage of the 'six doctrines'.

We have also mentioned Machik Labdron. She was a Tibetan who, in her youth, supported herself by reading the Prajñāpāramitā volumes. Patrons would employ her to read the texts aloud to gain merit, and she excelled at reading. (Not, as we might imagine in the West, because of the clarity and beauty with which she read, but because of her speed!) In reading these scriptures, she herself began to gain insight into the Perfection of Wisdom. Later she met an Indian teacher called Phadampa Sangye who taught her a form of the Chöd Rite. Out of her deep understanding, Machik developed a new form of Chöd which has since been incorporated into all Tibetan schools.

Siṃhamukha

The Chöd is a dramatized enactment of the principles of the Perfection of Wisdom. It is also a very powerful statement of faith in non-duality, and a test of your 'spiritual nerve'. To do it you go to an isolated, awe-inspiring place, such as a cremation ground. Then, after various preliminaries, you see your consciousness separate from your body and become a ḍākinī. The ḍākinī then chops what is now your corpse to pieces, and offers it, in a transmuted form, to all spiritual beings out of devotion, and to all mundane beings out of compassion. It is a particularly effective way of actualizing the 'spiritual ideas' of impermanence, insubstantiality, and non-duality, and attaining to a state of complete confidence in the Dharma, beyond hope and fear.

Machik Labdron, whose gift to humanity is the Chöd, is herself commonly shown as a white dancing ḍākinī – holding aloft a damaru in her right hand, and ringing a vajra-bell with her left.

Another famous woman *siddha* is Yeshe Tsogyal, one of the main disciples of Padmasambhava. After his disappearance to the Land of the Rākṣasas she became an important teacher in her own right. She was also responsible for writing down and concealing many of the termas left by Padmasambhava. These we could call 'Dharma time-capsules' – teachings that have been hidden in out-of-the-way places until they are needed. Padmasambhava is credited with the clairvoyant ability to see into future ages and teach the Dharma in forms suitable for the particular needs of those times. It is those teachings which Yeshe Tsogyal disseminated through Tibet. She is often shown in ḍākinī form, with a skull cup and a vajra-chopper.

The great guru Padmasambhava himself appears as a ḍākinī (which ought to dispel any fixed ideas we have of 'spiritual appearances' corresponding to physical sex). He appears as Siṃhamukha or Siṃhavaktrā ('lion-faced' or 'lion-headed' one, Tibetan *Senge Dongchenma*). She is a particularly powerful guardian ḍākinī, invoked in the exorcism of hindering forces. She is dark blue in colour, dancing with vajra-chopper and skull cup. Her head is that of a lion. Dwelling on Siṃhamukha should give us new insights into the nature of Padmasambhava.

The ḍākinī within

So far I have spoken of ḍākinīs as though they were externally existent beings, to be found in ancient Indian cremation grounds and the wildernesses of Tibet. But where is the real wilderness, the true cremation ground, to be found? Tilopa, in teaching Nāropa, repeatedly tells him:

> Look into the mirror of your mind...
> The mysterious home of the Ḍākinī.[59]

To understand how we can meet ḍākinīs within our own mind, we need to look more closely at what the ḍākinīs symbolize. In essence, ḍākinīs are all those experiences, internal and external, that inspire us and spur us on to practise the Dharma. Internally, the ḍākinī is all those outpourings of something higher and more spontaneous within us that make us feel we are on the right track, that we are making progress on the spiritual path. This does not mean that they are simply comforting. Occasionally they may be shattering, like lightning-flashes of insight that turn our view of ourselves and the world completely upside down.[60]

Whether we find the ḍākinīs' presence enjoyable or terrifying depends upon our degree of openness to them. If we meet them wholeheartedly, they come to us as feelings of inspiration, moods of great happiness and exhilaration, dauntless courage, sudden laughter, or total relaxation, the urge to give of ourselves completely, bursts of energy, poetry, and song. All these experiences on the highest level are gifts of the ḍākinīs. The ḍākinīs, you could say, are the muses of the transcendental.

Like the muses, the ḍākinīs are not controllable. They burst forth from higher levels of the mind (their 'mysterious home'). All we can do is create the right conditions for them to appear. We invite the ḍākinī and await developments. We do this mainly by Going for Refuge, committing ourselves wholeheartedly to the path, and doing our best to carry that commitment through.

However, I ought not to talk too blithely about inviting ḍākinīs. A word of warning: do not invite them unless you mean it. If you prove to be a fraud, or not to have the courage of your convictions – if you ostensibly commit yourself but then avoid the consequences – the ḍākinīs may leave you in disgust. (If we look at our lives we find that inspiration often disappears after we have ducked a challenge.) They may even threaten you – or that is how it may feel. If you are on the run from the Truth, on the run from your own creative energies, you will feel as though they are turning against you. You can end up feeling like a lion-tamer whose courage has left him, watching his lionesses jump off their stools and begin to close in on him....

Ḍākinīs do not stand on ceremony. Nor do they care about convention. They understand that all forms are Emptiness. They are the servants and messengers of the vajraguru. The Tantric guru is a desperado let loose in saṃsāra. He is prepared to do anything, however shocking, to save you from ignorance and suffering. So, as his agents, ḍākinīs are dangerous. Perhaps it would be better not to read about them unless you are prepared to take them seriously, to work at transforming yourself in line with what they ask of you.

Ḍākinīs are the unexpected, the spontaneous. They are the opposite of the safe security of one's ego prison. A ḍākinī may search for years (like Leonore for Florestan in Beethoven's 'Fidelio') seeking an opportunity to rescue you from the dungeon of craving and ignorance. When she suddenly appears in the darkness to cut you free from your shackles, you had better want to go with her.

To follow her is a risk. If you do, you will never be quite the same again. Ḍākinīs are wrathful and passionate. They always spell death for the ego. If you are ready, if you delight in her appearance and rejoice in her unpredictability, then you will find she gives death and birth. In exchange for suffering the blow of her vajra-chopper, you will experience a new and unimaginable freedom. She will then allow you to enter her dance, to dance into the fire, the flames of spiralling inspiration and ecstatic creativity. She will bestow her favours on you: wisdom, great bliss, the experience of non-duality, total liberation.

To start with, however, even though we may be committed and making an effort to practise the Dharma, the ḍākinī is likely to be elusive. For a while she appears in a certain spiritual practice, a certain Dharma teaching, a certain person even, and we feel enriched and inspired. Then she moves, shifts, changes shape. She changes her forms more often than a fashion-conscious woman changes her wardrobe. If you are attached to the forms she takes, the clothes she might wear, you will be left treasuring only a scarf or a shawl as a souvenir. The third of the ten fetters to Enlightenment enumerated by the Buddha was 'attachment to rites and rituals'. This does not mean that ritual has no place in Buddhism; the Buddha just denies that there is any point in going through the motions of any spiritual practice as an end in itself. This attachment to forms for their own sake is a kind of clinging to what the ḍākinī used to wear.

It is easy to become chained to particular aspects of spiritual practice. The wonderful meditation experience you once had can become a trophy, a party piece to trot out to impress your friends. A piece of Buddhist teaching which you have found helpful may become your dogmatic prescription for everyone. The ḍākinī, though, is reborn in every moment. She is in no particular form of practice or teaching. We have to strive to see her as she is in herself – the naked, voluptuous Truth. Once we have met her face to face in that way, she will appear to us in all forms. We shall recognize her unerringly in all aspects of existence, hear her crooning her song of the Dharma everywhere, for she is our own purified consciousness. To elaborate on Tilopa's advice, once the mind is a mirror, cleansed and spotless, then we shall see that it is 'the home of the ḍākinī'.

To arrive at this stage requires a great letting-go. The ḍākinī's halo of flames and total nakedness point to the burning off, the stripping away, of everything inessential. Higher states of consciousness are characterized by their total simplicity. To become one with the ḍākinī we have to follow the counsel of Padmasambhava:

> Let these three expressions: I do not have, I do not understand, I do not know, be repeated over and over again. That is the heart of my advice.[61]

Once this is achieved, you are the ḍākinī, the true free dancer in the limitless sky of Liberation.

The ḍākinī outside

I have said that the ḍākinī represents those inspiring forces which carry you along the path. Through visualizing a ḍākinī in meditation, you call up those energies within yourself. The difference between being in touch with the ḍākinī within and having to rely purely on your everyday energy to follow the path is like the difference between trudging across muddy terrain and hang-gliding above it. Hang-gliding is fast, free, exhilarating, and spiced with a certain risk. Without at least occasional flashes of inspiration, one can tire of the effort involved in painfully picking a path between the potholes. Thankfully, when your inner ḍākinīs refuse to come out to play (for ḍākinīs are playful – if they have gone away perhaps you have been too tense in your approach) there is still the possibility of deriving inspiration from an external ḍākinī.

We have seen that highly realized women can act as ḍākinīs. The tantras make much of finding a woman Tantric practitioner who is a ḍākinī (or, for women, of finding a ḍāka – a suitably qualified male sexual partner). Such women are said to have recognizable physical characteristics. The texts give detailed descriptions. On meeting with such a woman, the texts urge you to perform sexual yoga with her to further your realization. However, all this concerns the highly advanced Tantric practitioner. It has nothing to do with the satisfaction of mundane sexual desire, and for most of us this is so far beyond our present level and capabilities that it does not warrant thinking about. Unfortunately, there will always be people who bring their spiritual progress to a halt by assuming that they are ready for such practices when they are still light-years distant from the necessary degree of attainment. It is very easy to fool oneself that one is engaging in sexual yoga, and that one's partner is a ḍāka or ḍākinī, when really one's feet are still set in the concrete of craving.

Assuming that we are not highly advanced Tantric adepts, and do not have the good karma to meet a highly realized partner, can we find a ḍākinī outside? We have seen that the Tantra, in its pragmatic way, tries to find equivalents to the spiritual in our experience. So the guru becomes the esoteric (or 'directly experienced') Buddha Refuge. The ḍākinī is the esoteric Sangha Refuge – the hidden ruby of the Sangha. The purpose of the sangha is to inspire and encourage us along the path. The visualized ḍākinī, the ḍākinī within, has this function. However, we can also see whether there is some fellow practitioner of the Dharma who inspires us.

We may find the sangha in general inspiring, but for the Tantra this is not enough. The esoteric Refuges are personal. We could even call them the 'intimate' Refuges. They are the aspects of the exoteric Refuges with which we feel a direct link, and to which we have made an individual commitment. Though sangha members may be encouraging and helpful, that does not qualify them to be our ḍākinī Refuge. However, if there is a fellow Dharma practitioner with whom we have direct personal communication, and whose company and example stir up our energy to practise the Dharma, then for us that person acts as a ḍākinī. They may be a man or woman, sixteen years old or eighty, no matter. The criterion is that in their presence we call up more energy for our efforts to follow the path. They wake us up. They get us moving.

If we find such a person, it is no good sitting around hoping they will be our friend. We just have to commit ourselves to being a friend to *them*. If we are active, giving to them and helping them, then if they have that ḍākinī quality they will respond.

Once again, as with the inner ḍākinī, we had better mean it. Spiritual friendship (Sanskrit *kalyāṇa mitratā*) is demanding. It is fuelled by authentic communication. It is close; there are strong feelings involved. Nonetheless, there can hardly be anything so deeply satisfying, and so pleasurable, as a spiritual friendship with someone who for us has that ḍākinī quality.

In such a friendship, people work to remove any barriers between them. They let go of thinking of their own needs, of fear of self-revelation and intimacy. They try to let go of everything and give themselves to the Dharma, to a mutual exploration of the Truth. They take delight in that Truth, knowing that they are together in this evanescent form so briefly that their meeting has never been before and never will be again, and that in the moment they are both unknowable. When two separate individuals are united in the Dharma, there we find the play, the true dance, of the ḍākinīs.

The Four Great Kings

Seven

The Dark Armies of the Dharma

Avalokiteśvara, the Lord of Compassion, gazes out across the world, his white radiance soothing the sufferings of living beings. With one pair of hands he clasps to his heart the wish-fulfilling gem of his vow to eradicate the world's pain. In his upper left hand he holds the lotus of spiritual receptivity, the desire to leave the mud of saṃsāra and reach up towards the sun of true happiness. Above his head we sense the oceanic love of Amitābha, his spiritual father. In Avalokiteśvara's heart the mantra *oṃ maṇi padme hūṃ* rotates ceaselessly, pouring its light into the six realms of suffering.

In his upper right hand we see his crystal mālā turning. With each bead another being's sufferings are extinguished. We watch the dancing reflections in the crystal beads, follow their steady rhythm as aeons pass.

Still the beads flow through the milk-white fingers. The pace is steady, smooth, ceaseless. And yet ... there is still so much agony, pain, and frustration mirrored in those patient eyes. Hearts which hear the call of the mantra and long to respond are chained by dark forces, restrained by fear, bewildered by confusion, so that they do not know whence the sound comes or how to follow it.

The sapphire eyes cloud with a gathering storm of spiritual impatience. They steal a glance at the steady, but too slow, circling of the crystal beads to their right. They look once more, hard, at the plague forces of ignorance, the jailers of hatred, the ransomers of craving who hold so many beings in their clutches.

The crystal beads begin to change shape. They lose their sparkling reflections for a sun-bleached white. They become a death's head garland, a rosary of skulls. The delicate white hand grows darker, its light changing from white to deep blue, like an eclipse of the sun. The powerful hand's first and last fingers stab the air in a menacing gesture. Around it roars a corona of flames.

With a world-shaking cry the figure, now blue-black, starts to its feet. The wish-fulfilling jewel transforms into a vajra-chopper and a skull cup dripping with red nectar. The soft lotus transforms into a trident with a death's head. From the huge, overpowering blue-black body another arm thrusts out, rattling a skull drum. To the left a further fist uncoils a noose.

The giant figure pounds forward, wild hair streaming upward, tied round with snakes. The massive body, nearly naked, girt only with a tiger-skin, wears skulls – pretty, staring skulls – as jewels. Snake-enwreathed, fang-mouthed, three eyes glaring bloodshot from an awesome face, he marches onward bellowing challenge.

Answering his call, legions of similar figures pour from the empty sky, forming fiery ranks behind him. Thigh-bone bugles summon ever more misshapen Dharma champions out of the ten directions. To the left of the leader, a devil's cavalry of furies appear. Female figures, unkempt and dangerous, riding on horses, riding on goats. Their leader sits side-saddle on a mule, brandishing weapons, wreathed in fire, her fanged face contorted in fury. As she rides, her feet drum on the flayed human corpse that hangs from her saddle.

The dark army hurtles forward and enters the kingdom of Māra, the custodian of saṃsāra. Māra's sentinels see them coming, their warning cries freezing with horror in their throats. No alarm is needed though, for the clashing of the weapons, the pounding of the hooves of that terrible horde, and the battle-cry of their leader causes earthquakes in all six realms, and shakes the foundations of Māra's palace.

Māra's imperial guard, sent out to do or die, hesitates in its first charge, flinging down weapons that would only serve to slow its headlong retreat. Māra's daughters, sent to parley, are dumped unceremoniously over the backs of the advancing cavalry, their alluring dresses dragging in the mud.

Regiments of hatred are routed. The artillery of fear is overrun. Poison clouds of envy and doubt just cause the attackers to grow larger and stronger. In his last stronghold, Māra holds all sentient beings hostage, threatening to take everything down with him. It does him no good. The deepest dungeons of the hells, their walls thick as ignorance, are taken by storm.

The bone mālā in the huge right fist whirls so fast now that no skulls can be seen. It is just a perfect circle of white light. As the hostages are led out, free at last, the eyes of the giant black general look down at them with fathomless compassion.

Mahākāla ('great black one', Tibetan *Gonpo Nakpo Chenpo*) is the wrathful manifestation of Avalokiteśvara. He is a *dharmapāla* (Tibetan *Chokyong*) – a 'protector of the Dharma'. We have already met Yamāntaka, the wrathful manifestation of Mañjuśrī, as well as the wrathful form of the serene young Bodhisattva Vajrapāṇi. In Tantra, the most benign and peaceful figures can also assume the most horrifying and powerful forms. The greater your love for sentient beings, the more total will be your movement against whatever harms or threatens them. With total selflessness you have an unhesitating, fearless response to their needs.

Dharmapālas are often visualized along with the three esoteric Refuges. They do not form a fourth Refuge, rather they are the vajra-wall of protection that guards the three Refuges, both exoteric and esoteric. They are the bodyguards of the Tantra. They defend its teachings and its practitioners from inner or outer enemies. As is typical of Tantra, their protective power is understood and used on many different levels.

Dharmapālas are invoked for magical protection from external harm by some Tantric practitioners. Namkhai Norbu Rimpoche tells how he used a sādhana of the dharmapālas to give warning of attacks by bandits when making a dangerous journey across Tibet.[62] Tibetan monasteries had a special shrine-room for the performance of dharmapāla rituals. The monks assigned to the practice sat in the darkened room, their texts illumined only by the butter lamps on the shrine. In the gloom they could discern the images of the Protectors. The room would be strewn with old weapons donated to the monastery. Carcasses of wild beasts adorned the ceiling. In this awe-inspiring and forbidding place the monks would chant the rituals that protected the area from misfortune, from sickness, and from storm. Their rites, it was believed, cast a circle of protection over the region.

On a deeper level, dharmapālas throw back into the shadows the forces of nightmare and madness which always threaten to tear loose and subjugate the human psyche. On the group level, these forces unleash hatred, war, holocaust, and the destruction of art, culture, and religion. Breaking free in the individual they are psychosis and megalomania. They are the forces of rape and pillage, slaughter and sadism, chaos and dissolution. Finally, they are the forces through which men and women destroy themselves, by which humanity breaks its toys and plunges itself into darkness or oblivion.

These dark and unregenerate forces, the shadow beasts of the psyche, are firmly debarred from entering the mandala, so the dharmapālas also appear as gatekeepers in mandala rituals. On the principle of 'set a thief to catch a thief' they appear in menacing forms, more terrifying than the dark horrors they guard against. They stand four-square in the jewelled gateways of the mandala, preventing any negative emotion from disturbing its harmony.

Dharmapālas guard the secrets of the Tantra from idle disclosure to the uninitiated. They protect Tantric practitioners from breaking their vows and pledges. They can be summoned up by the yogin or yogini when intractable forces in their personality threaten to pull them off the path. They also warn against the ugly states into which advanced practitioners who leave the path can fall. Not for nothing are Tantric practitioners sometimes cautioned that with initiation they are bound either for Enlightenment or the worst hell.

The dharmapālas do not simply stand sentry. They move outwards, extending the boundaries of the mandala. They go on the offensive, subduing and transforming the foes of the Dharma. Their weapons and emblems are taken from the dark hordes they have pacified and disarmed. In particular, they have defeated the Māras and Rudra. For Buddhism, Rudra is the personification of the furthest excesses of selfishness. He is the ego gone supernova, ignorance run rampant. (Chögyam Trungpa called him the ultimate spiritual ape.) He is represented as a vast, grotesque figure, brandishing weapons. Pig-ignorant, plug-ugly, he uses the sheer force of his greed and self-centredness to bludgeon his way to power. He is a child's tantrum universalized. In the *Life and Liberation of Padmasambhava* he is humbled and subdued by the wrathful Vajrapāṇi and the dharmapāla Hayagrīva.

This symbolism is interesting. The ego, in its attempts to make the world secure for itself, finally bumps into Reality. For the ego, Reality is a threat against which it constantly tries to erect defences, only to have them flattened, sooner or later, like card houses. As a rigid defensive structure, the ego can only see Reality in its own terms, as a more powerful force, a demon that will destroy it. If you 'go with' the Dharma, allow the gentle influence of the Bodhisattvas to soften you, then your open heart experiences the Three Jewels as beautiful and peaceful. If you struggle and resist, then they are dangerous. This is why, in the *Tibetan Book of the Dead*, after the dead person fails to recognize the peaceful deities and escapes from them, wrathful deities appear. It is as though the bardo-being is all the time experiencing the Clear Light of his own consciousness, but in an increasingly alienated way. First there is the Clear Light itself. From a slight distance of separation, the beginnings of the fall back into duality, the Clear Light of Reality is perceived as the peaceful forms of the Buddhas and their retinues. At a greater distance Reality seems to take on menacing, terrifying forms. It is as though, having tried gently to coax you to it and failed, your Buddha-nature communicates a warning. It tries to head you off from more suffering. If you recognize the true nature of the wrathful deities, you are instantly Enlightened. If you keep on running, you find yourself back on the treadmill of the six realms.

In Tantra, the dharmapālas embody a still further set of meanings. We have seen that Tantra sees the world and its inhabitants in terms of energy. Because of this vision, it finds nothing to reject. Nothing is too horrible, too evil. Every emotion, even the most negative, represents a unit of energy to be harnessed for Dharma practice. It is just a question of finding the appropriate skilful means to turn poison into wisdom. The dharmapālas represent the energies of anger, even hatred and violence, put at the service of the Dharma. Tantra turns anger into vajra-anger. Now powered not by egotism but by inner compassion and serenity, the aggressive impulses of the psyche are channelled into destroying ignorance and suffering.

Tantra is Buddhism in the Underworld. It teaches the Dharma to our shadow sides, to the gnomes and hobgoblins of our unconscious, adopting forms and apparel familiar to the denizens of those inner territories. Just as we saw that, with mudrā, Tantra takes Buddhism to our fingertips, through the dharmapālas it takes the golden message of the Enlightened Ones into the darkest underground troll-chambers of the mind.

The dharmapālas are a source of courage for Tantric practitioners, standing by them in their spiritual struggles and sounding warning notes if they stray from the path. More than that, by visualizing dharmapālas in meditation, Tantric practitioners can connect with the fearlessness of the Enlightened Mind and rally the energy required to break through to new levels of awareness.

However, when meditating on these wrathful guardians, Tantric practitioners must beware of falling into mere mundane anger. They have always to bear in mind that, though of outwardly terrifying aspect, the dharmapālas are inwardly serene and gentle. They are manifestations of the most beneficent forces imaginable. Their fierce power is subordinate to the great love and compassion of the Bodhisattva.

Within the spiritual community, with their vajra brothers and sisters, Tantric practitioners can manifest as ḍākinīs, totally open and loving, joining in the dance within the mandala. Venturing out into the dark alleys of unbelief, striding the corridors of power, they don the spiritual armour of awareness, patience, and energy. Then the ḍākinī may transform into a dharmapāla.

Spiritually-minded people are sometimes expected to be meek and mild-mannered. Buddhism values true gentleness, but it also thinks highly of heroism and clear thinking. You may approach a Buddhist teacher with some clever intellectual question only to have your words crumpled up and thrown back at you. You may find your vague generalizations and woolly rationalizations hacked to pieces before your eyes. To the ego, the teacher may appear at times like a larger ego, shooting you down in flames, so completely self-assured that you may feel he or she is not open to your viewpoint. However, the teacher may just be defending the Truth, quite selflessly, from your attempts to sabotage it.

The certainty of a true spiritual teacher comes not from fixed views but from their own insight into Reality. They are unshakeable. They may even get angry, which can be terrifying. They can mobilize more aggressive energy than ordinary people because they are much more concentrated. At times you may feel seared by the burst of fire directed at you. You may realize only later that the vajra hurled in your direction left you unscathed. It simply shattered some of the chains which bound you, leaving you freer than before.

The dharmapālas are also a reminder to the practitioner that the dark side of life is an expression of Reality, just as much as the light and beautiful. Recognizing the wrathful forms as aspects of Buddhas and Bodhisattvas makes it easier to see difficult or frightening situations as expressions of śūnyatā. The dharmapālas represent the way the Tantric practitioner accepts the challenge of painful life events, and by becoming one with them transforms their nature. We have come across the suggestion that work is a Tantric guru. For the alert disciple, all situations, whether seemingly good or bad, can be their guru. They can all be used as opportunities to deepen insight and strengthen compassion.

Dharmapālas are of two kinds. First, there are emanations of the *dharmakāya*, such as Mahākāla, whom we saw hurtle into action at the beginning of this chapter. Then there are mundane entities, known as lords of the soil, who have been converted to the Dharma. The combined total of these two classes of dharmapālas within the Tibetan tradition is several hundred, if not more. The Dalai Lama has discouraged Westerners from involving themselves with meditations on mundane protectors. He feels they are inappropriate to the Western situation.[63] Most of us are still at the stage of learning to relate to the most central figures of Buddhism: the Buddhas and Bodhisattvas, gurus and yidams.

Mahākāla

It would not be helpful to become caught up with sādhanas of figures which, while they can exercise a fascination for some people, are of comparatively minor importance for spiritual development. In the rest of this chapter we shall look at a few of the most important Tantric protectors individually.

Mahākāla

Mahākāla is the most commonly invoked of all Dharma protectors, and is important to all schools of Tibetan Buddhism. In Tibetan he is often known simply as 'the Lord'.

He has over seventy different forms, and each particular school has those it particularly favours. For the Nyingmapas it is the Four-Faced Lord; for the Karma Kagyu the squat, misshapen Black-Cloaked Lord. For the Sakyapas it is the Lord of the Tent, whose special emblem is a magic staff resting across his outstretched arms. For the Gelukpas the most important form is the six-armed, whom we have already seen in action, holding the skull rosary in his upper right hand. He is also invoked in major gatherings of the Geluk monastic assemblies in a four-armed form.

This 'hastening six-armed' form is usually shown trampling on the prostrate form of Ganesha, the elephant-headed Hindu god. Chögyam Trungpa suggests that Ganesha symbolizes subconscious thoughts. When we lapse into distraction and mental chatter, Mahākāla stamps out our subvocal gossip, and calls us back to attentiveness. Though there are Mahākālas of different colours, they are typically huge, blue-black, and tremendously wrathful. They are often surrounded by a retinue of similar figures, or by other demons and demonesses. A good example of such a visualization is given in a sādhana of the Four-Faced Lord.

This form of Mahākāla is blue-black, with faces to the right and left of the central one, and one above. The front one is black, and munches a corpse. The others are each of a different colour and expression: wrathfully smiling, roaring with laughter, and frowning. All have three glowering eyes, which see into the past, present, and future.

He has four arms. Each performs one of the four karmas, or actions, which is the main task of this Mahākāla. These are (1) to subdue sickness,

Śrīdevī

hindrances, and troubles; (2) to increase life, good qualities, and wisdom; (3) to attract whatever Dharma practitioners need and bring people to the Dharma; and (4) to destroy confusion, doubt, and ignorance.

His inner left hand, close to his body, holds the skull cup of nectar. Here, this represents Emptiness and pacification. In his inner right hand he carries a hooked knife, representing skilful means and the power of increasing. His upper right hand wields a sword, which performs the function of attracting. His upper left hand waves a trident spear, for destroying craving, hatred, and ignorance at one thrust.

Wreathed in crackling flames, his body encircled with writhing snakes, and skull-crowned, his right foot stamps down hard on a prostrate figure, representing egotism. From his inner left forearm dangles a mālā of skulls, and in the crook of that arm is a pot of wine. His fanged faces glare out, their beards and eyebrows blazing like the fire which will consume the universe at the end of the aeon.

Around him is his retinue. First come the four Mothers: black Ḍombinī, green Caṇḍālī, red Rākṣasi, and yellow Siṃhalī, on his four sides. All are naked, with vajra-choppers and skulls of blood. Their bodies emit fire, and they visit plagues on enemies of the Dharma and those who break their Tantric vows. Beyond them march measureless hosts of protectors and the eight classes of demons, as well as twenty-one knife-wielding butchers, each with a retinue of a hundred thousand similar figures. The Dharma army fills the earth and sky.

O Mahakala and the seventy lords in your retinue,
Yours is the power to overcome all Maras
And to carry on high the victory banner of Dharma.
Yours is the power to bring joy to the world.[64]

Śrīdevī

The female companion of Mahākāla, whom we saw riding into battle alongside him and who equals him in power, is Śrīdevī ('glorious goddess', Tibetan *Paldan Lhamo*). Just as Mahākāla is the 'dangerous' form of the benign Avalokiteśvara, so Śrīdevī has both peaceful and wrathful forms. Her peaceful manifestation is known as Ekamātri Śrīdevī

(Tibetan *Machik Paldan Lhamo*). Dressed in celestial clothing, she sits on a lotus in the posture of royal ease, her left foot slightly extended. She wears a Bodhisattva crown of jewels, and smiles compassionately. In her left hand she holds a bowl filled with jewels. In her right hand is a standard with pennants in all the colours of the rainbow. Her body is enhaloed with brilliant light.

In her wrathful guise she is somewhat different. She is dark blue, ferocious, with three bloodshot eyes. Her flaming red hair stands on end, and above her head is a fan of peacock feathers. She has sharp fangs, and laughs with a sound like thunder. She rides on a mule, which is galloping furiously over a sea of blood. It is said that she is riding towards Siberia, after an unsuccessful attempt to convert the king of (Sri) Lanka to the Dharma. Her mule has been hit by the vengeful king's arrow. The wound in its flank has been transformed into a wisdom eye.

She is largely naked, her body wreathed with snakes and adorned with bone ornaments and a necklace of skulls. In her left hand she bears a brimming skull cup. In her right she holds aloft a black skull-topped command staff. Flames roar and black storm-clouds swirl around her as she gallops along. From her saddle hangs a pouch with dice. (Her initiation is held to be a gateway to divinatory powers, and she can be invoked by practitioners of *mo*, the Tibetan system of divination, which involves the use of dice. There is also a lake called Lhamo Latso, to the south-east of Lhasa, whose reflections are said to reveal the future.) She sits side-saddle on the flayed skin of her own son.[65]

According to a tradition quoted by Alice Getty, Śrīdevī was given various gifts by other deities. She received the dice from Hevajra in order to determine the life of men. She received the fan of peacock feathers from Brahmā (one of the most important Hindu gods, who was incorporated into Tantric Buddhism as a minor protector). Vajrapāṇi gave her a hammer, and various other deities gave her a lion and a serpent, which she wears as earrings, and her mule, which has deadly snakes for reins.[66]

Śrīdevī brandishes her staff to threaten all obstacles to the success of the Dharma. Her terrible form serves as a warning of the fearsome states into which Tantric practitioners may fall if they fail to keep the pledges taken at the time of initiation. Tantric practitioners also acknowledge that the meditations they practise enable them to accumulate a great deal of psychic power. A person who engages in advanced Tantric practice but no longer feels bound to use the power he or she has gained for ethical purposes is thus a great danger both to themselves and to others. Someone who uses the power derived from a Tantric sādhana to gratify their own ego rather than laying it at the service of all sentient beings is basically engaging in black magic. Figures like Śrīdevī have the power to subdue those who abuse their power and render them harmless.

Not only can she control dark external forces; Śrīdevī is capable of pacifying all those hindering inner forces that bind us to the 'wheel of fire' of mundane existence. Hence she is also known in Tibetan as Paldan Makzor Gyalmo ('one who overpowers and crushes the hosts of the passions'). The tradition that she is seated on the skin of her own son suggests perhaps her complete overcoming of all attachment, for of all emotional connections that between mother and child is probably the strongest.

There are many forms of Śrīdevī, and different schools of Tibetan Buddhism may regard one or another of them as their special protector. Her meditation was introduced into Tibet by Sangwa Sherap, and to begin with she played an important part in the practice of the Sakya school. In the fifteenth century she was 'appointed' Dharma protectress of Ganden, one of the great Geluk monasteries, by the first Dalai Lama. Ever since then she has been a special protectress of the Dalai Lamas. The fifth Dalai Lama wrote instructions for meditating upon her, and a *thangka* of Śrīdevī travels with the Dalai Lamas wherever they go. For centuries this *thangka* was kept unseen in its red case, but in 1940 the present Dalai Lama, then aged about seven and on his way to be enthroned, was met close to Lhasa by a great crowd of officials and notables, including his three main servants, one of whom had brought the *thangka*, hidden as usual in its case. On seeing it near the entrance to his tent, he promptly grabbed it, took it inside, and opened it. The *thangka* which had not been unveiled for so long was revealed. The Dalai Lama surveyed it and then replaced it in its case. Everyone present was amazed by what he had done.

Like Mahākāla, Śrīdevī has a retinue, one so large that Blanche Christine Olschak says that a description of this alone would fill a whole iconographic book. It includes the four Queens of the Seasons, the five Goddesses of Long Life, and twelve goddesses known as *tanrungmas*. These are indigenous Tibetan deities who have been converted to the Dharma, and now guard and protect the practitioners of various meditation lineages.

Śrīdevī also has in her retinue a type of female protectress known as *mahākālī*. They are generally mounted on horses or mules, with goatskin bags of poison hanging from their saddles. They have bows and arrows, and lassoes made of snakes. They each wear a mirror, in which all one's karma is reflected. They are swift-acting and ferocious against enemies of the Dharma.

The Nyingma protectors

The Nyingma school is the oldest form of Buddhism in Tibet and calls on many protectors rarely or never invoked by other schools (though the Drukpa Kagyu also invoke the Nyingma protectors). Many are believed to have been converted to the Dharma by Padmasambhava, who in his travels subdued the demons and spirits he encountered in the mountains and other wild places. He subjugated entities hostile to the Dharma by the power he had gained through Tantric practice, forcing them to tell him their seed syllable, their true name, and then binding them by oath to be servants and warriors of the Dharma. In this way, many of the indigenous gods and demons, the Pans and Draculas of Tibet, were converted to the Dharma.

Because they are native to Tibet, these figures can take on very different shapes to that of the Mahākāla type of figure. Padmasambhava must have been totally fearless, for these Nyingma protectors appear in some of the most horrific forms imaginable. They are such stuff as nightmares and psychotic hallucinations are made on. They are your worst fears, the creatures you knew were lurking in the darkness when as a child you hid under the bedclothes but could not sleep. They make the rats in Orwell's Room 101 seem like angels. Nonetheless, while commanding a healthy respect from their devotees, these strange figures call forth reverence and devotion in the Tantric practitioner, in the same way as do the benignly-smiling Buddhas. They take many forms, too many to list, and too much to encounter. It will be enough to meet just three of them, who form a group known in Tibetan as *ma za dam sum*.

First comes Rāhula, known to Tibetans simply as Za. He is half serpent, half what we shall have to call humanoid (though any woman giving birth to such a horror would not survive the experience sane). He coils his lower body over the corpse of ego. His upper body is huge, black, and covered with a thousand eyes, all of which glare balefully. In the pit of his stomach is a cavernous mouth which, with the eyes on his upper body, give the feeling that his whole torso is a massive glaring face. He has nine heads, arranged in three tiers of three, each with three bulging eyes. A great breath of sickness issues from their fanged mouths. From the crown of the topmost head sprouts the black, cawing head of a raven.

A human skin is draped over his back. He is wreathed in snakes and adorned with scorpions. In his right hand writhes a sea-serpent, in his left is a bow and arrows, which he fires unerringly at those who break their religious vows. There is no concealment from him as his thousand eyes see your every thought.

In ancient Indian legend, Rāhu was a titan who disguised himself and tried to steal nectar from the gods. He was exposed by the sun and moon, and Vishnu cut off his head. However, he lived on in the sky, where he became the dragon's head.[50] Rāhu avenged himself on his betrayers by periodically swallowing them – he is the lord of the eclipse. Consequently he is sometimes depicted as a reddish-blue deity holding the sun and moon in his hands.

Rāhula is the destroyer of Rāhu. Just as Yamāntaka took over the attributes of Yama, Lord of Death, so Rāhula assumes those of Rāhu to protect the Dharma by threatening its enemies with eclipse. His dark body with its myriad eyes is reminiscent of the starry night sky. The gaping mouth in his belly represents the swallowing of sun and moon.

For Tantric yogins, the eclipse of sun and moon can have an esoteric significance. One of the principal aims of Tantric yoga is to eclipse all craving and hatred by bringing the energies which usually flow in two psychic channels (associated with the sun and moon) into the central psychic channel (Sanskrit *avadhūtī*).

In the lives of the eighty-four great *mahāsiddhas*, we find the story of an old man called Rāhula, who complains that the full moon of his youth has been swallowed by the Rāhu of old age. He gains advanced Tantric realizations following the instructions of a yogin, who sings to him:

> When the dragon of non-dual realization
> Eclipses the subject/object circle of constructs,
> ... then the qualities of the Buddhas arise.
> Ehma! Immortality is so wonderful![67]

Za is also known as the lord of lightning. As a Dharma protector, he strikes the enemies of the teaching with epileptic fits and madness. (Popular Tibetan tradition holds that the shadow of Rāhula's raven's head falling upon you causes apoplexy.) Then he devours them, cramming their carcasses into the gaping maw in his belly. This is just one of his forms....

If Za was rather overpowering, and you thought a female guardian might be less formidable, I am afraid you are going to be disappointed. The next of the group of three is Ekajaṭā (or Ekajaṭī) (goddess with 'a single plait of hair', Tibetan *Tsechikma* or *Ralchikma*). In fact, singularity, or the uncompromising vision of things from the highest viewpoint, seems to be the message of this figure. She too is dark and menacing, flame-enhaloed, nearly naked. Her skull-crowned hair writhes upwards. Her face contorts with fury. Her brows are knitted and she has but one eye, in the middle of her forehead. From her ugly mouth protrudes a single fang. She is often depicted with only one breast. She is wreathed in severed heads. With her right hand she waves a stake on which is impaled a live human figure. In her left hand she displays the heart of a foe of the Dharma, which she has ripped out. She is the supreme protectress of the Dzogchen teachings, the highest and most precious of all Nyingma practices. She also functions as a guardian of mantras – preventing them being disclosed to those unworthy to use them, and ensuring that those who have been empowered to use them do so for appropriate purposes.

She may perhaps guard them in a more general sense as well, preventing them losing their power and efficacy, or from being lost altogether.

As with all the dharmapālas we have met, Ekajaṭā can assume a number of forms and colours. Characteristically she is dark brown, though she can also be red or blue. Her different forms hold various implements or weapons. One scholar describes forms holding a trident, a heart, and a snare; a trident and skull cup; or the heart of an enemy and a 'clever falcon'. She can also, on occasion, dispatch numerous female wolves as messengers.[68]

Ekajaṭā also appears, in a slightly less terrifying form, as an attendant on Green Tārā, along with red Mārīcī, the goddess of the dawn. In this context she has two eyes and so forth, and holds a vajra-chopper and a skull cup, and is described as 'sky-blue, wrathful but loving and bright'.[69] By an extension of this role, she came to be seen as a kind of blue form of Tārā, known as Ugrā Tārā, or Tārā the Ferocious.

The third member of this fearsome triad is Vajrasādhu ('oath-bound diamond', Tibetan *Dorje Lekpa*, sometimes shortened to *Dorlek*). He is considered by those brave souls who have encountered all three of these protectors to be the most approachable. His aid is sometimes enlisted in relatively mundane matters, whereas Rāhula and Ekajaṭā are uncompromisingly concerned with threats to the Dharma on the highest level.

Vajrasādhu is a pre-Buddhist Tibetan deity, defeated by Padmasambhava, who bound him and his 360 companions by oath to protect the Dharma. He is most easily recognized by his round, wide-brimmed helmet. He is usually depicted riding on an animal. One common form is red, mounted on a lion, fully clothed, with a skull cup in his left hand. In his right hand he holds aloft a vajra, which he wields with a penetrating gesture.

The environment in which Vajrasādhu is represented as appearing is in keeping with his appearance. In one text it is described as follows:

> Surrounded by the wild sea of blood lies a castle built of bat-bone, from which a five-coloured rainbow emanates. Up in the sky, poisonous

> clouds gather and a terrific storm, accompanied by fiercely rolling thunder and by the flashing of meteors and lightning, rages there.[70]

Vajrasādhu has a rather sinister emanation known in Tibetan as *Garpa Nakpo*. This figure is blue-black, seated astride a 'snarling goat'. In his right hand he brandishes a flaming bronze hammer, in his left he holds a blacksmith's bellows. The horns of the goat twist around each another, suggesting the way in which the dualities of relative truth are transcended when one sees things from the viewpoint of absolute truth.

The four gatekeepers and the four Great Kings

One of the major functions of dharmapālas is to act as guardians of the mandala. Generally the mandala palace has four doorways, and in many mandalas these are guarded by four gatekeepers (Sanskrit *dvarapāla*). They stand in the entrances to the mandala, preventing any hindering force from entering. They also have the effect of blocking your retreat if you should lose heart once you have entered the mandala. We shall take as an example the mandala of the five Buddhas as described in *A Guide to the Buddhas*, the first book in this series. In the *Tibetan Book of the Dead*, along with other peaceful deities who form the Buddhas' retinue, four wrathful deities appear as guardians of the gates. They are the white Vijaya ('victorious'), the yellow Yamāntaka ('slayer of death'), the red Hayagrīva ('horse-necked one'), and the green Amṛtakuṇḍalin ('swirling nectar').

Of these, Yamāntaka and Hayagrīva are important both as dharmapālas and as personal deities (yidams). We have already met Yamāntaka in Chapter Five, so we shall concentrate here on Hayagrīva. As the guardian of the western gate, Hayagrīva (Tibetan *Tamdin*) is the particular protector of the Lotus family of Amitābha. Hayagrīva is an Indian deity whose Tantric practice was brought to Tibet by Padmasambhava. His recognition symbol is a green horse's head (occasionally there are three of them) protruding from his flaming yellow hair. The horse is neighing wildly in a voice that shakes the three worlds. The horse's head commemorates Hayagrīva's part in the subjugation of Rudra, ego run rampant, which is described in the life-story of Padmasambhava. Hayagrīva transformed himself into a horse, and entering the vast body of Rudra by the anus forced him to surrender. This incident demonstrates the extremely humiliating and deflating shock that awaits the overblown ego when it encounters Reality. It is not eternal; it cannot control the world. It has to learn humility and a sense of perspective.

The deities we have looked at so far are all of the transcendental order, symbolized by their standing on lotuses. There are other forms of protector, known as *lokapālas*, who are not expressions of Enlightened consciousness but are invoked as powerful mundane forces, sympathetic to the Dharma and caring for its practitioners. Perhaps the most important of these are the Four Great Kings.

In art, these kings are commonly shown in full armour. They are sometimes standing, sometimes seated in 'royal ease'. Their leader, the King of the North, is Vaiśravaṇa (Tibetan *Namthore*), yellow in colour, holding a cylindrical banner in his right hand, and a jewel-spitting mongoose in his left. In the east, the white Dhṛtarāṣṭra (Tibetan *Yulkhorsung*) plays a lute. To the south the green Virūḍhaka (Tibetan *Phak Kye po*) holds a sword. In the west, the red Virūpākṣa (Tibetan *Mikmizang*) holds a stupa, or reliquary, in his right hand, and a snake, or nāga, in his left. They each head a great retinue of living beings, such as gandharvas (celestial musicians) or yakṣas (powerful mountain spirits).

The energy of these lokapālas is less overpowering than that of the dharmapālas. They are the beneficent forces at the summit of the mundane who, while not themselves Enlightened, are receptive to the influence of the Buddhas and Bodhisattvas. They encourage the good in the world, helping to perpetuate the Dharma, and encouraging its influence to spread. For instance, in chapter 6 of the *Sūtra of Golden Light* they come forward and promise to protect those who propagate the sūtra, and in chapter 14 of the *Vimalakīrti Nirdeśa* they undertake to protect whoever reads, recites, and explains it.

The order of reality of the dharmapālas

In this chapter we have encountered a class of figures who can be quite overpowering in their ferocity, and terrifying because of the atmosphere of nightmare darkness that surrounds them. Nonetheless, they are all protectors of the Dharma, and are emanations of Emptiness in the same way as the peaceful forms of Buddhas. Because they are apparently so threatening, it can be tempting to explain them away as merely symbolic. Before doing so, we might pause to consider the testimony of Namkhai Norbu Rimpoche concerning depictions of dharmapālas:

> Though the iconographic forms have been shaped by the perceptions and culture of those who saw the original manifestation and by the development of tradition, actual beings are represented.[71]

A Śākyamuni Refuge Tree (from a sādhana written by Sangharakshita)

Eight

The Refuge Tree and its Future Growth

In the course of this series of books we have opened the treasury of the Buddhist tradition and encountered the immense riches of its symbolism. It is now time to bring together all the figures we have encountered into one unifying symbol, and to contemplate the totality of the facets of the jewel of Enlightenment.

Tibetan Buddhism has such a unifying symbol, known variously as a Refuge assembly, Field of Merit, or Refuge Tree. It is known as a Refuge assembly because it is a visualized gathering of figures representing the three Refuges. It is known as a Field of Merit because by visualizing a great array of Enlightened figures and then making offerings to them, and by performing other skilful actions, such as committing oneself to the Bodhisattva path in their presence, one gains for oneself a great deal of positive benefit. For Buddhism, thought and imagination are forms of action, and will have positive or negative consequences depending on their motivation. The Tantra takes this to its logical conclusion. When performed with faith and devotion, it sees no inherent difference between making offerings to a hundred Buddhas visualized in meditation and doing so in the outer world. It is known as a Refuge Tree because the assembly is often visualized seated upon a vast lotus flower, with many branches at different levels.

It is possible to visualize a Refuge Tree with any yidam at its centre. Whichever yidam you are concentrating on, you can build up a visualization of all the Refuges with that figure as the central focus. It is even possible to perform a condensed version of the meditation by visualizing just the central figure while maintaining the firm conviction that it is the embodiment of all the Refuges. This figure is sometimes called the *saṃgrahakāya* or 'comprehensive body', as it is the synthesis of all objects of Refuge.

The general appearance of the Refuge Tree is similar for all schools of Tibetan Buddhism – all the Refuges, exoteric and esoteric, are ranged in the sky around a central figure who is understood to embody them all. However, each school has one or more forms of Refuge Tree, each of which synthesizes all their main teachers and lineages of meditation practice. It is as though each school had gone to its treasury of spiritual practice and laid out its finest jewels on display in the sky: as well as embodiments of the exoteric Refuges, there are its greatest scholars and yogins, the yidams whose meditations are most central to it, and the ḍākinīs and dharmapālas with whom it has a special connection.

To visualize such an assembly, perhaps including hundreds of figures (if one has the skill to produce such a masterpiece in one's mind's eye), or even to see a well-executed *thangka* of it, can be quite breathtaking. The sheer number of figures, their richness and variety, and the feeling of the different aspects of the Dharma they embody and express, can have a profound effect on the mind.

Each Refuge assembly is both individual and universal. It is a vehicle through which a Tibetan Buddhist can develop faith and appreciation for the particular school of practice that he or she has joined, and its distinctive traditions of spiritual practice. At the same time, each assembly includes figures representing all the Refuges, both exoteric and esoteric. Thus, although they may depict different figures, each Refuge Tree is a complete symbol of all the aspects of the human psyche raised to the highest pitch of perfection. Within each assembly all our energies are illuminated by the golden rays of Enlightenment, and find themselves included in one great harmony.

As a paradigm for the Refuge Tree we shall look at the Nyingma version, and then go on to consider the differences in emphasis in some of the other schools. We shall also consider the meditational contexts in which these vast assemblies are visualized and, finally, reflect on how they may develop further in the West.

The Nyingma Refuge Tree

For the last time, we shall enter the vast blue sky of śūnyatā, allowing ourselves to let go of worries and concerns, to drop all limiting concepts, and to expand into the freedom of the unchained mind.

In the midst of that vast blueness appears a cloud made of rainbow light, pouring its rays into the surrounding sky. Out of this multicoloured cloud grows the stem of a great white lotus flower. Seated on the lotus, his body blazing with light, is Guru Padmasambhava – the source of the Nyingma tradition. He is dressed as a king of Zahor, as we saw in Chapter Four, wearing the three royal robes, holding a golden vajra and a brimming skull cup, and with his khaṭvāṅga in the crook of his left arm. The only differences here are that he is seated cross-legged in the vajra posture, and his right hand does not rest on his right knee but clasps the vajra to his heart.

Growing out from the central lotus towards the four cardinal points are four more lotuses. On the lotus closest to us, in front of Padmasambhava, is a great assembly of Buddhas of the three times – past, present, and future. At their head is Śākyamuni, the Buddha of our own age. He is flanked by Dīpaṇkara and Maitreya. Dīpaṇkara was the Buddha who, long ago, predicted that Śākyamuni would gain Perfect Enlightenment. He is usually depicted in monastic robes and wearing a pandit's cap. Maitreya is the Buddha who will rediscover the path to Enlightenment after the teaching of Śākyamuni has died away.

On the lotus furthest away from us, beyond Padmasambhava, is a great heap of books of the Dharma: sūtras, tantras, and commentaries. They are all wrapped in precious silks, and radiate light and the sound of the Dharma in the form of teaching and mantras.

On the lotus to the left of Padmasambhava as we look at it is a great assembly of Bodhisattvas. They are all young and attractive, dressed like Indian princes and princesses, wearing the jewels and silks that symbolize the beauty of their practice of generosity and the other Perfections.

Samantabhadra and Samantabhadri

Their bodies emit brilliant light, and surging waves of love and compassion. They are headed by Avalokiteśvara, Mañjuśrī, and Vajrapāṇi.

On the lotus to our right are the great arhats, the enlightened disciples of the Buddha. They are of various ages, dressed in yellow monastic robes, and each holds a begging-bowl and the wanderer's staff. They are headed by Śākyamuni Buddha's chief monastic disciples, such as Śāripūtra, Maudgalyāyana, Mahākāśyapa, and Ānanda.

The Buddhas of the three times, books of the Dharma, Bodhisattvas, and arhats are the embodiments of the Three Jewels in their exoteric form. However, there are yet more figures. The great white lotus on which Padmasambhava sits has three tiers of lotus petals, on which the esoteric Refuges appear in brilliant ranks.

On the tier immediately below Padmasambhava sit the great gurus. The usual practice is to have on this tier those teachers with whom one has a personal connection, by dint of having received teaching or initiation from them. Then in the sky around Padmasambhava appear the gurus of the past, especially those who preserved and transmitted the teachings that one practises. So we see a great assembly of saintly monks, scholars in pandit's caps, wild-looking yogins, and other people through whose practice and efforts the Dharma has come down to us. Each of them, out of immense kindness, has become an embodiment of the Dharma in their own lives, and made sure that the treasures of Buddhism would be preserved for future generations. They are the living links, forming the golden chain which connects us to the Buddha – a chain that has continued unbroken for two-and-a-half millennia.

On the next tier of the white lotus, below the gurus, appear the great yidams of the four classes of Tantra. These include one or two of the figures we met in Chapter Five, as well as some other yidams specific to the Nyingma tradition. The figures of the Highest Tantra are mainly swathed in flames, clasping their consorts in the close embrace that symbolizes the union of skilful means and wisdom. These figures are the esoteric Dharma Refuge.

On the lowest tier are the ḍākinīs and dharmapālas. The ecstatic ḍākinīs dance wildly, full of the blissful inspiration of the Dharma. Prominent

Vajradhara

among them in the Nyingma Refuge Tree will be Siṃhamukha, the lion-headed, blue ḍākinī form of Padmasambhava. Along with the ḍākinīs are the dharmapālas – the protectors of the teaching, headed by the three chief Nyingma protectors: Ekajaṭā, Rāhula, and Vajrasādhu.

In the sky directly above Padmasambhava sits Garab Dorje, dressed as a *mahāsiddha*. He is the founder of the Dzogchen lineage, a form of practice that claims to go beyond schools and the three yānas. However, many of its most important practitioners have been Nyingma teachers. Above him in the sky is Vajrasattva, radiant white, holding the vajra to his heart and a vajra-bell to his left side. Finally, at the zenith, in a sphere of light, sits the *adi*-Buddha Samantabhadra (Tibetan *Kuntuzangpo*) – symbol of the ever-present potentiality for Buddhahood which is inherent in the universe, beyond space and time. He is naked and unadorned, his body deep blue in colour. He is seated in sexual union with his white consort, Samantabhadri.

In the vast prairies of the sky around the Refuge Tree, gods and goddesses are making delightful offerings to Padmasambhava and all the Refuges.

Refuge Trees of other schools

We have seen that each school of Tibetan Buddhism has a Refuge Tree tradition which is its centre of practice, common to all followers of that school. The general principle of the arrangement will be similar for all schools – all the Refuges, exoteric and esoteric, are ranged in the sky about a central figure who is understood to embody them all.

For the Kagyupas the central figure is usually the *adi*-Buddha Vajradhara. He is deep blue in colour, seated in full-lotus posture. His hands are crossed in front of his heart. In his right hand is the vajra, in his left the vajra-bell. Kagyu Refuge Trees always give prominence to the lineage of gurus we met in Chapter Four: beginning with Tilopa (who was directly inspired by Vajradhara), and continuing through Nāropa, Marpa, Milarepa, and Gampopa. They are also likely to show Cakrasaṃvara and Vajravārāhī prominently positioned among the yidams.

For the Gelukpas the central focus is Je Tsongkhapa, the founder of their school. He is dressed in monastic robes and the yellow pandit's cap, holding the stems of lotuses which bloom at his shoulders, supporting the flaming sword and book, which denote that he is considered an emanation of Mañjuśrī. In his heart the figure of Śākyamuni Buddha is often to be seen. (One also finds Geluk Refuge assemblies whose central figure is Śākyamuni, with Vajradhara at his heart.)

Geluk Refuge Trees tend to be less obviously lotus-like than those of other schools. Usually the central figure sits on a lotus in the sky with figures on a many-tiered lotus below him. In the sky above and to each side of him are ranged a mass of gurus, so that the overall impression is of a kind of cruciform arrangement around the central figure.

In the sky above Tsongkhapa are great gurus from whom the Geluk school particularly draws its inspiration, including a number of Indian *mahāsiddhas*. To the left, as we look, is the Bodhisattva Maitreya, usually represented with a white stupa or chorten as his emblem. To the right is Mañjuśrī, with the flaming sword and book. They are both surrounded by a sea of gurus. Together they represent the Method and Wisdom lineages respectively, the teachings dealing with compassionate activity and the realization of Emptiness, which were synthesized by Atīśa, whose tradition the Gelukpas continue.

Below Tsongkhapa is a great array of figures on a many-tiered lotus. On the highest tiers are the yidams of Highest Tantra such as Yamāntaka, Cakrasaṃvara, Guhyasamāja, Kālacakra, Hevajra, and Vajrayoginī. Beneath them appear other figures associated with the three lower classes of Tantra. These tend to be serene and peaceful, as opposed to the flame-encircled Anuttarayoga yidams. On the succeeding tiers sit a calm array of Buddhas. A set of thirty-five Buddhas is often depicted. These are associated with a practice of confession used by those who have taken the Bodhisattva vows, based on a passage in the *Upāli-Paripṛcchā Sūtra*. A set of seven Buddhas, known as Manuṣi Buddhas (Tibetan *Sangye Rapdun*) are often included too. These are Buddhas of past epochs. They are all seated in full-lotus posture, wearing monastic robes, and can be distinguished by their hand-gestures. Vipaśyin has both hands on his knees, palms inwards, fingers reaching down in the earth-touching mudrā.

Śikhin holds his right hand up in front of him in the *vitarka* mudrā of victorious argument, while his left rests in his lap. Viśvabhū holds his hands in the gesture of turning the Wheel of the Dharma. Krakucchanda has his right hand on his knee, palm outwards, in the *vārada* mudrā of supreme giving; with his left hand he grasps a fold of his monastic robe. Kanakamuni has his hands in the same positions as those of Buddha Śikhin. Kāśyapa has his left hand in his lap, while his right makes the mudrā of supreme renunciation, known as the *Buddha śramaṇa* mudrā. The seventh of these Buddhas is Śākyamuni, the Buddha of our current age.

Also frequently included in the assembly of Buddhas is a set of eight Medicine Buddhas (Tibetan *Menlha Deshek gye*). These Buddhas, who are particularly venerated for their healing powers, are led by the Buddha Baiṣajyaguru or Baiṣajyarāja (Tibetan *Menlha*). Though he is sometimes represented as golden in colour, his characteristic colour is blue. Indeed he is also known as Vaiḍūryaprabharāja ('king of lapis lazuli radiance'). His left hand rests in his lap in the mudrā of meditation, supporting an iron begging-bowl. His right hand is at his right knee, palm outwards, offering a sprig of the myrobalan plant (Latin *terminalia chebula*), a healing fruit well-known in Indian medicine. His retinue consists of six other Buddhas who are his brothers in healing, and Śākyamuni Buddha, the Buddha of our epoch, who is sometimes referred to as the Great Physician because he has taught the Dharma, which is the antidote to the sickness of suffering within saṃsāra. (The Four Noble Truths may even be based on an ancient Indian medical formula of diagnosis, cause, prognosis, and treatment.)

The Medicine Buddha appears in contexts other than the Refuge assembly. In Indian Buddhism there is a tradition of meditation on a mandala of fifty-one figures, of which he is the central one. He also became an important figure in later Chinese Buddhism. According to Raoul Birnbaum,[72] the most common set of figures on the principal shrine in large Chinese monasteries consists of Śākyamuni flanked by Amitābha to his right and Baiṣajyaguru to his left (which is symbolically the east, the direction in which the Pure Land of the Medicine Buddha is said to be located).

Below the Buddhas are commonly depicted eighteen arhat disciples. These are a set of sixteen arhats mentioned in Indian tradition, with the addition of their two attendants, Dharmatala and Hva-shang. These disciples of Śākyamuni are credited with having spread the Dharma all over India, up into the Himalayas, and even to the Karakoram. Each has his own individualized iconography.

Finally, on the lowest tiers of the great lotus, come the ḍākas, ḍākinīs, and dharmapālas. Among the dharmapālas, particular prominence is given to Mahākāla and Śrīdevī.

Below the great lotus stand the Four Great Kings. The lotus is a symbol of the total abandonment of saṃsāra, so only those who have entered upon the transcendental path are represented enthroned on a lotus flower. The kings are commonly shown in full armour. The dharmapālas who are emanations of the *dharmakāya* generally scorn all protection, frequently going naked.[73] They are immune to being affected by anything mundane, for they have seen right through to its true, illusory nature. However, the lokapālas, though they stand at the summit of mundane existence, still need to protect themselves from its slings and arrows.

The Refuge Tree and Going for Refuge

We have now looked briefly at the Refuge Trees of some different schools of Tibetan Buddhism. Now that we have seen them, the question arises, how are we going to relate to them? There are several ways to do this. Some people appreciate them simply on an aesthetic level, looking at them in the way in which an art student might examine a painting in a museum. Those who are interested in Jungian psychology often see them as expressions of the Jungian archetypes. The gurus and arhats are aspects of the Wise Old Man, the ḍākinīs are anima figures, the dharmapālas shadow figures, and so on. However, relating to a Refuge Tree in either of these ways is not to relate to it as a Refuge Tree at all. It only becomes a Refuge Tree when you go for Refuge to it.

Going for Refuge, committing yourself to the path to Enlightenment, is not something you do only once. Rather, it has to be repeated over and over again, as you develop. Through doing so, you acknowledge the

Refuge Tree not just as an exotic picture but as a blueprint for what you can become – a vision of all the energies of your psyche transmuted and put at the service of the highest possible ideal. This vast array of figures represents the ocean of the unfolded wisdom, compassion, and energy of Buddhahood. If you make the effort to develop the potential inherent in every man and woman, it is a display of the riches of the treasure-house of your own mind. Recognizing this, you keep on committing yourself, ever more deeply, placing more and more reliance on the Three Jewels, until you yourself have become the path, and embody the Three Jewels in yourself.

One traditional meditation for deepening and strengthening this commitment is the Going for Refuge and Prostration practice (which, as we saw in Chapter Three, is one of the Foundation Yogas). In this practice you begin by visualizing the Refuge Tree in the sky in front of you, with all the Refuges, exoteric and esoteric. In addition you visualize your father and all men to your right, your mother and all women to your left. Any enemies you may have are in front of you, and your friends are ranged around immediately behind you. In this way you generate the feeling that you are not committing yourself to gain Enlightenment for yourself alone. Part of the Enlightenment experience is the realization that you are not inherently separate from other beings, so how can you aim to emancipate yourself from the wheel of suffering and leave them still trapped? Hence, from the Mahāyāna point of view, your aspiration to gain Buddhahood must be based on a deeply felt desire to do so in order to be of maximum usefulness to all sentient beings. The Tantric approach, as we have seen, is to make ideals as concrete as possible, so it urges you not just to feel the desire to take all beings with you on the path, but actually to do so imaginatively. Thus you visualize all other beings also committing themselves to the path to freedom around you.

In most forms of the practice you next recite a short verse expressing your aspiration to go for Refuge to the guru, the Buddha, the Dharma, and the Sangha, until you have attained Enlightenment. Not only this, you imagine all other sentient beings wholeheartedly reciting the verse with you.

Then you make full prostrations[74] to the visualized Refuge Tree, each time reciting another verse expressive of your Going for Refuge to all the Refuges. When this practice is performed as part of the Foundation Yogas it is customary to perform a set number of prostrations every day, until you have accumulated a total of 100,000. At a rate of 100 a day, this will take three years to complete, so it is quite a commitment of energy.[75]

If you perform the practice regularly, the effect is very definitely cumulative. The more time you spend with this great vision of all the attributes of Buddhahood, the more the energies of the depths of your being are stirred. After a while, you start to feel that with each prostration you are throwing yourself more deeply into the spiritual life. To start with it feels awkward; most Westerners are not used to expressing strong emotion. The idea that you should feel such devotion for something that you would just want to throw yourself face down in front of it is a strange one for us.

However, the more you do, the more natural it becomes. The stiffness of pride and the ingrained feeling that you often find in the West that 'nobody is any better than me; my opinion is as good as anyone else's', gradually dissolves away. You feel extremely happy and fortunate to be living in a universe in which there are beings much wiser and more loving than you. It becomes a relief to have an ideal to which you can aspire, for it is not an unattainable goal to which you are prostrating. There is a path which, step by step, prostration by prostration, you can follow. As you follow it, you become more fulfilled. Life gains deeper meaning. More than that, you begin to have something to offer to other people. You feel yourself part of the solution to the world's difficulties, rather than part of the problem.

As you carry on, launching yourself forward in the direction of Enlightenment, even more happens. Your feeling of being a solid self, building up a rather sketchy mental image, changes. You begin by describing the whole thing to yourself artificially: 'the ḍākinīs should be on this tier', and so on. You feel as though you are playing a game, painting a picture. With time, though, the figures in front of you come to have a greater and greater effect. You feel yourself in the presence of something. You feel less that you are creating a picture, and more that you are contacting another level of reality.

Gradually, the great array of figures may take on at least as much reality as the 'I' which is supposedly creating them. The reality they embody is shining, brilliant, loving, wise. The distance between you and them steadily decreases. Finally, you feel no separation at all. You become your own refuge. You understand that all these figures are simply expressions of aspects of the Enlightened Mind. In experiencing those states for yourself, the path comes to an end. In realizing the same states of mind as the Buddhas, Bodhisattvas, and great gurus, you and all of them, in the graphic language of Zen, 'breathe through one nostril'. At this point there is nothing to do but work for other living beings – who are no longer conceived of as 'other' or 'separate'. In Going for Refuge more and more deeply, you have become the Refuge Tree.

Future developments

Throughout this series of books I have tried to describe the Buddhist figures as they have been handed down by tradition. At times I have ventured to suggest personal associations with them, or interpretations that are not traditional, but I have not made any changes to their iconography. The question we now have to ask is: will these figures change further with time, and with their introduction to the West?

There seem to be two extreme views about this. Some people, of whom Carl Jung is probably the best known, have argued that Buddhist iconography cannot take root in the Western psyche. Jung thought the Eastern Buddhist figures too alien to be happily accepted into the unconscious of Westerners. He favoured making the best of Christianity, rather than transplanting Eastern figures into Western spiritual development. I personally think that if Jung had lived longer, he would have revised his judgement. When I first came into contact with Buddhas and Bodhisattvas I found it took very little time before I was dreaming about them and happily meditating upon them. I did not find them so strange and alien that I could not emotionally connect with them. In some ways their unfamiliarity was an advantage. As they were not familiar from my childhood I had no particular associations with them and could come to them afresh. Their 'otherness' seemed appropriate, for they symbolized a reality of which I had no experience at all. It was as though they came from a golden land I had never visited. The inhabitants of such a wondrous realm should not look like ordinary people.

As time has gone on, I have come to know hundreds of other people who found it quite easy to make an emotional link with the Buddha and Bodhisattva figures, and even the ḍākinīs and dharmapālas. I am in contact with hundreds of people who meditate on them and do not encounter any real cultural or psychological barrier to accepting them. The figures 'work' for them.

At the other extreme are those people who are convinced of the value of the tradition, and feel that the sādhanas should be practised unchanged in the West. They are not open to any further developments. For me, there has to be a middle way between these two extremes. A tree is an organic and growing thing. So the Refuge Tree is not set in a fixed and final form. It can still change, develop, and put out more branches. Its figures can transform into new shapes. Once you understand its essence, you will see that Reality can be expressed through an ocean of different forms. In communicating your experience to other people, under new conditions, you may well find new figures appearing.

Before we see the appearance of *new* figures, we are more likely to find different juxtapositions and combinations of the traditional ones. One way in which this may happen is through a breaking down of sectarianism within Western Buddhism. When Buddhism has come to a new part of the world, a fresh synthesis has often been brought about which has drawn on teachings and practices from a number of different schools. This happened, for instance, in China, where the T'ien T'ai school was essentially a synthesizing school, bringing together several different elements. So there is no reason in principle why new Refuge Trees that incorporate not just figures from the Indo-Tibetan tradition but from other parts of the Buddhist world should not appear in the West.

This widening-out beyond the boundaries of traditional schools happened to a limited degree in Tibet in the nineteenth century. A number of renowned lamas of different schools, concerned about the dangers of sectarianism, started swapping their lineages of initiation and practice. Thus was born a movement known as Ri-me (without boundaries, pronouned *ree-may*), which has continued up to the present day. However, there is no reason why the concept underlying the Ri-me movement should not be more widely applied. Why should one not dissolve away all the boundaries between Buddhist schools? Clearly one needs to use a limited number of methods, and to follow a consistent set of instructions, otherwise one will not make much progress. It is hopeless to try to be a Tibetan Buddhist, a Pure Land follower, and a Zen practitioner all at once. Nonetheless, while for practical purposes we have to narrow down our field of concern, there is the danger that in doing so we limit our sources of inspiration, or even develop narrow-minded allegiance to one school. It is important that we feel and understand that the essence of Buddhism is Going for Refuge, and that we ourselves stand shoulder to shoulder with all those who have done so, no matter what their school or lineage.

As an example of a direction that Buddhism in the West could take, I shall mention aspects of a Refuge Tree that appears in a new sādhana introduced into the Western Buddhist Order by Sangharakshita. This tree has Śākyamuni at its centre, as the source of the entire Buddhist tradition and to emphasize the common parentage of the entire family of Buddhist schools and traditions. As usual, there are figures representing all the Refuges. What is different about this Refuge assembly is that the spiritual teachers represented do not come from just one, or even several, schools of Tibetan Buddhism. It includes figures such as Padmasambhava, Milarepa, and Tsongkhapa, but in addition there are teachers from many other Buddhist traditions. For instance, there are great masters from the Zen tradition: Hui Neng, Dōgen, and Hakuin. This Refuge assembly, then, emphasizes the underlying unity of the Buddhist tradition. In Going for Refuge to it one acknowledges the various expressions of the Buddhist tradition under different circumstances as different ways in which human beings have followed the same Dharma of the Buddha, and moved in the direction of the same Enlightenment. One recognizes that one is first and foremost a follower of the Buddha and only secondarily a member of a particular Buddhist school. Thus the practice is a strong antidote to sectarianism.

Even though this new Refuge Tree incorporates figures not found in the Tibetan tradition, it does not introduce any new iconographic element into Buddhism as a whole. The spiritual teachers from different countries are all visualized following traditional representations. As time goes on, however, I am sure that there will be changes in the forms of Buddhas, Bodhisattvas, and Tantric deities, just because they are being depicted or visualized by Westerners. I have friends who are artists, who paint and sculpt Buddha and Bodhisattva figures. They adhere to the tradition, and yet ... they are Westerners, and one can see that their work expresses their Westernness. Faces become less oriental; one can see the influence of great Western artists in the style of their painting and sculpture. I have no doubt that this is how new forms will gradually emerge. Western artists and meditators do not need to try to produce figures appropriate for the West. We just have to pour ourselves wholeheartedly into the traditional forms. Once we have become deeply imbued with the spirit of the tradition, once we have begun to see beyond their forms to the Reality of which they are an expression, then changes will naturally occur. Over perhaps a few generations, completely new figures will emerge. In future, Western Refuge Trees we shall find, as well as new manifestations of Buddhas and Bodhisattvas, and Western men and women among the ranks of the spiritual teachers.

So this series of books will never be finished, once and for all – or at least not as long as there are people practising the Dharma, and exploring the golden realms of higher states of consciousness. What I have written is only a summary of the story so far. Now that the Dharma has come to the West, we have the opportunity to unfold still further the rich tapestry of Buddhist symbolism by making contact with the beautiful archetypal figures of the Buddhist tradition, going for Refuge to them, and making them our own through meditation and devotional practice. Then through our meetings with the Buddhas, Bodhisattvas, and Tantric deities, we shall be able to add further chapters to this book, to reveal more of the treasures to be found in the storehouse of the human mind.

Notes

1 The Buddha often stayed at the Vultures's Peak (Gṛdhrakūta) from where he delivered many discourses. It is on a hill near Rajgir in Bihar, and now a major Buddhist pilgrimage site.

2 The Nyingma school counts six levels of Tantra: *kriyā, upa-yoga, yoga, mahā-yoga, anu-yoga*, and *ati-yoga*. For a schematic sketch of these, see Professor G. Tucci, *The Religions of Tibet*, Routledge and Kegan Paul, 1980, pp.76–81.

3 This is not the only possible arrangement of the five Buddhas in the mandala. To generalize, in most of the earlier tantras and in the practices of the Nyingma school, Vairocana is at the centre, while many of the later tantras, including the Highest Tantra practices of the other main Tibetan Buddhist schools, have Akṣobhya as the main figure.

4 For a very full account of these channels, winds, and drops, see Geshe Kelsang Gyatso, *Clear Light of Bliss*, Wisdom Publications, 1982, chapter 1.

5 *Yab-yum* is an honorific term. The ordinary Tibetan for 'father-mother' would be *pha-ma*.

6 *The Tibetan Book of the Dead*, Trungpa and Fremantle translation, Shambhala, 1975, p.60.

7 I am here quoting the slightly amended version of the sonnet, published under Keats's supervision in 1817. I have followed the punctuation given in *John Keats – The Complete Poems*, ed. John Barnard, Penguin, second edition, 1977.

8 On the first of his three trips to India, Marpa the Translator (see Chapter Four) was carrying with him many precious texts previously unknown in Tibet. His travelling companion, Nyo of Kharak, was jealous of Marpa's more valuable haul from their sojourn in India. As they were being ferried

across the Ganges he bribed someone to throw Marpa's texts into the river. See *The Life of Marpa the Translator*, trans. Nalanda Translation Committee directed by Chögyam Trungpa, Prajna Press, 1982, pp.36–42.

9 See *The Perfection of Wisdom in 8,000 Lines and its Verse Summary*, trans. Edward Conze, Four Seasons Foundation, 1973, p.9.

10 In his hasty enthusiasm, Keats may be forgiven for getting his facts confused. The first European to view the Pacific from the New World was not Cortéz but Balboa. Furthermore, he was not rendered speechless by the experience, but gave vent to the typically Spanish exclamation 'Hombre!'

11 In this description of the development of the Prajñāpāramitā literature I am following the view of Edward Conze. Some Japanese scholars place the *Diamond Sūtra* somewhat earlier.

12 See *Heart of Wisdom*, Tharpa, 1986, pp.156–63.

13 Edward Conze's translation, in *Buddhist Wisdom Books*, Unwin, 1988, p.115.

14 According to B. Bhattacharyya this form is known as Kanaka Prajñāpāramitā. (See *The Indian Buddhist Iconography*, Firma klm Private Ltd., 1987, p.199.)

15 The individual parts of the mantra can be assigned meaning, or at least have connotations, but it is not really possible to build from these a 'translation' of the mantra as a whole.

16 When chanted in Tibetan monasteries and Dharma centres, this mantra is often prefaced with *tadyathā oṃ*. *Tadyathā* (often pronounced *tayatā* by Tibetans) means 'it is like this'.

17 See, for example, Geshe Rabten, *Echoes of Voidness*, Wisdom, 1985, pp.43–4, and *Heart of Wisdom*, Tharpa, 1986, pp.132–3. As with so much Tibetan teaching, they are here following earlier Indian Buddhist commentaries, some of which can be found in Donald S. Lopez Jr, *The Heart Sutra Explained*, State University of New York Press, 1988.

18 The exact list varies from school to school. The main meditations are: (1) Going for Refuge and Prostrations, (2) Generating the Bodhicitta, (3) Vajrasattva purification, (4) Offering the Mandala, (5) Guru Yoga. The Nyingmapas frequently talk of the four Foundations, with the Guru Yoga becoming a further practice. The Kagyupas usually amalgamate Going for Refuge and Bodhicitta, hence producing a different set of four. The Gelukpas add further preliminaries to make a total of nine. (See the books by Jamgon Kongtrul, Geshe Rabten, and Khetsun Sangpo Rinbochay in the Selected Reading for this chapter.)

19 See, for example, the *Tharpe Delam – The Smooth Path to Emancipation*, part of a larger Nyingma meditation manual. A translation by Michael Hookham was published by Kham Tibetan House, Saffron Walden (n.d.), under the title *The Bliss Path of the Liberation of Mahā-Ati Meditation*.

20 The understanding that one has a Buddha-nature outside time must not be taken as an excuse for inaction. It is not good enough to sit back thinking, 'I am already Enlightened'. We still have to realize this truth directly through our own efforts to go for Refuge.

21 The wording of the mantra in Sanskrit and its translation into English both present problems. After some thought, I have here used a version by Dhammachari Sthiramati. It does not follow any of the Tibetan ways of chanting the mantra, but makes good sense of the Sanskrit. After comparing nineteen different texts, he makes a persuasive case for his version in *The Order Journal*, issue 3, published privately, November 1990, pp.60–73.

22 Without the *hūṃ phaṭ*, the mantra as given here has exactly one hundred syllables.

23 For an explanation of the meaning of 'skilfulness' in Buddhism, see the Glossary entry for karma.

24 Quoted in Roshi Philip Kapleau, *Zen: Dawn in the West*, Rider, 1980, p.184.

25 While this is generally true, the Tantric tradition is aware of the danger of this situation being exploited by gurus who are 'not what they ought to be'. There are usually safeguards which enable the disciple to decline to follow any advice of the guru that would go against the Dharma. There is a particularly helpful discussion of the guru–disciple relationship by the fourteenth Dalai Lama in chapter 3 of his commentary to the third Dalai Lama's *Essence of Refined Gold*, trans. Glenn H. Mullin, Snow Lion, Ithaca N.Y. 1982.

26 Padmasambhava even has his own Pure Land, known as the Glorious Copper-Coloured Mountain (Tibetan *Zangdok Palri*).

27 For an authoritative discussion of the history of the various traditions of Vajrakīla see Dudjom Rimpoche, *The Nyingma School of Tibetan Buddhism, Its Fundamentals and History*, Wisdom Publications, 1991, vol. 1, pp.710–16.

28 In describing the symbolism of this form of Padmasambhava, I am largely following the oral commentary of Sangharakshita. For a valuable interpretation which differs from mine in many details, see that of Dilgo Khyentse Rinpoche in *The Wishfulfilling Jewel*, Shambhala, 1988, pp.21–4.

29 'Eternity' in *Poems From The Notebook, 1793*. See *Blake – Complete Writings*, ed. Geoffrey Keynes, Oxford University Press, 1969, pp.179 and 184.

30 For an account of this incident, see Nam-mkha'i snying-po, *Mother of Knowledge*, trans. Tarthang Tulku, Dharma Publishing, 1983, pp.71–2.

31 This was the ḍākinī Vajrayoginī. See Chapter Six.

32 See *The Life of Marpa the Translator*, trans. Nalanda Translation Committee directed by Chögyam Trungpa, Prajna Press, 1982, p.198.

33 See *The Hundred Thousand Songs of Milarepa* in Selected Reading.

34 *The Jewel Ornament of Liberation*, trans. Herbert V. Guenther, Rider, 1970. This is an important Lam Rim text. (For a discussion of Lam Rim, see the section on Tsongkhapa later in this chapter.)

35 See Keith Dowman, *Masters of Mahāmudrā*, State University of New York Press, 1985, p.46.

36 Set out in Atīśa's *Bodhipathapradīpa – A Lamp For the Path to Enlightenment*. See Richard Sherburne's translation in *A Lamp for the Path and Commentary*, Allen and Unwin, 1983.

37 Geshe Wangyal, *The Door of Liberation*, Wisdom Publications, 1995, p.141.

38 I want again to express my thanks to Graham P. Coleman of the Orient Foundation for confirming that these five yidams of Highest Tantra (along with Vajrayoginī, whom we shall meet in the next chapter) are the ones on which most teachings have been given by Tibetan lamas in the West. However it is with regret that considerations of space have prevented me from examining deities associated particularly with the Nyingma tradition, such as Vajrakīla.

39 All this is rather complex. David Snellgrove gives a very succinct explanation: '*Śambara* and *saṃvara* represent the same name in Sanskrit with slightly variant spellings, but the second spelling happens to be identical with the word meaning a vow or a bond. Thus the Tibetans translated them differently: *Śambara* as *bDe-mchog [Demchog]*, "Supreme Bliss," which is how they interpret this name, whatever the spelling, and *Saṃvara* as *sDom-pa [Dompa]*, understood as "binding" or "union". The compound name, Cakrasaṃvara, is therefore interpreted as the "union of the wheel and the elements" explained in various ways, but suggesting in every case the blissful state of perfect wisdom.' David L. Snellgrove, *Indo-Tibetan Buddhism*, Serindia, 1987, p.153.

40 The attributes of these deities vary depending on the particular lineage of instructions you follow. They may be two- or four-armed. Bhairava may hold a cutlass and staff or other emblems instead of the knife and skull cup.

41 For example, Tibetan Buddhists consider that Cakrasaṃvara has his abode on Mount Kailash (Tibetan *Gang Rimpoche*), a mountain in south-western Tibet. Hindus consider this mountain to be the throne of Shiva.

42 More literally this means 'joined in a pair'.

43 While Vajrabhairava is always classified as a yidam of the Father Tantra, Tsongkhapa in his *Lam Rim Chenmo* says that Vajrabhairava sums up all Father and Mother Tantras and has iconographical aspects not found in any other tantra.

44 This incident is the twenty-ninth case in the koan collection known as the *Mumonkan* or the 'Gateless Gate'. There are several translations in English. See, for example, *Two Zen Classics: Mumonkan and Hekiganroku*, trans. Katsuki Sekida, Weatherhill, 1977.

45 Raphael Henry Gross (ed.), *A Century of the Catholic Essay*, Ayer Publishing 1971, p.233.

46 There is another classification system, used mainly by the Sakyapas, that adds a third category of non-dual tantras, which balance method and wisdom. According to this system, Hevajra and Kālacakra (discussed below) are both considered non-dual tantras.

47 David L. Snellgrove, *Indo-Tibetan Buddhism*, Serindia, 1987, p.156.

48 Nairātmyā is commonly the consort of Hevajra, though in certain sādhanas his consort may be Vajravārāhī (Cakrasaṃvara's consort) or Vajraśṛṅkalā (diamond chain).

49 Or, in some traditions, a lion.

50 In traditional Vedic astrology, the north lunar node is called the dragon's head (Rahu), and is considered an eighth planet, the other seven being the Sun, Moon, Mercury, Venus, Mars, Jupiter, and Saturn.

51 The Tibetan historian Buton (1290–1364) gives a different account, in which it was Vajrapāṇi who taught the Tantra to Indrabhūti. His kingdom then became a huge lake full of nāgas, to whom Vajrapāṇi gave the Tantra for safe keeping. The nāgas wrote it on golden leaves with lapis lazuli, and later passed it on to a ḍākinī.

52 The mandala of Mañjuvajra is the first in the important collection known as the 'Niṣpanna Yogāvalī'. In this, Mañjuvajra is vermilion red and six-armed. With his central pair of arms he embraces his consort, and in the others he holds a sword, arrow, lotus, and bow.

53 This is the Vajrayāna name for what in hatha yoga is known as *padmasana* – the full-lotus posture.

54 The initiations the Dalai Lama gives are known as the 'seven initiations in the pattern of childhood' and authorize practice of the generation stage of Kālacakra, involving visualization of the mandala. There are a further eight initiations in the Kālacakra system, which empower one to practise the advanced meditations of the completion stage.

55 Although this is the traditional view, there is no scholarly evidence for this or any other tantra having been taught by the historical Buddha during his lifetime.

56 The exact tally depends on how you count. Are the *yab-yum* figures one or two? However you do it, the total is impressive. Lokesh Chandra makes it 634, Jeffrey Hopkins manages to reach 722.

57 In Tantric practice ḍākas and ḍākinīs are sometimes referred to as heroes (Tibetan *pawo*) and heroines (Tibetan *pamo*).

58 For examples of rituals involving Kurukullā see Stephan Beyer, *The Cult of Tara*, University of California Press, 1978, pp.301–2. I suggest that some of them perhaps come a little close to black magic not because they are performed for an unskilful purpose (though taken out of context they could be), but because they are attempts to use magic power to coerce people or spirits against their will.

59 e.g. Herbert V. Guenther, *The Life and Teaching of Nāropa*, Oxford University Press, 1963, p.67.

60 For these reasons, Guenther has described ḍākinīs as 'ciphers of transcendence', a phrase borrowed from the Existentialist philosopher Karl Jaspers. See Herbert V. Guenther, *Tibetan Buddhism Without Mystification*, E.J. Brill, 1966, p.103.

61 Yeshe Tsogyal, *The Life and Liberation of Padmasambhava* (2 vols), Dharma Publishing, 1978, canto 93, p.635.

62 *The Crystal and the Way of Light – The Teachings of Namkhai Norbu*, compiler and ed. John Shane, Snow Lion, 2000, p.128

63 The Dalai Lama discusses this in the *Bodh Gaya Interviews*, Snow Lion, 1988. See pp.76–8.

64 From 'A Prayer to Mahakala' by the first Dalai Lama, trans. Glenn Mullin, in *Selected Works of the Dalai Lama I*, second edition, Snow Lion, 1985, p.199.

65 Here I am following *The Gods of Northern Buddhism* by Alice Getty (Charles E. Tuttle, 1962), who bases some of her account of Śrīdevī on Schlagintweit's *Buddhism in Tibet*. According to Getty, in one of her previous lives Śrīdevī was married to the King of the Demons (yakṣas) in Ceylon (Sri Lanka). She vowed that she would convert them to the Dharma or wipe out the royal race. When she failed to interest her husband in the Dharma she 'flayed her son alive, drank his blood, and even ate his flesh'.

66 Ibid., pp.149–50.

67 Keith Dowman, *Masters of Mahāmudrā*, State University of New York Press, 1985, p.253.

68 See de Nebesky-Wojkowitz, *Oracles and Demons of Tibet*, Mouton, s'Gravenhage 1956. pp.33–4.

69 In 'Praise of the Venerable Lady Khadiravaṇī Tārā Called the Crown Jewel of the Wise' by the First Dalai Lama, *In Praise of Tārā*, trans. Martin Willson, Wisdom Publications, 1986, p.302.

70 Quoted in *Oracles and Demons of Tibet*, op.cit., p.157.

71 *The Crystal and the Way of Light* (see Note 62), p.129.

72 Raoul Birnbaum, *The Healing Buddha*, Rider, 1980, pp.90–1.

73 One exception is the Dharmapāla Bektse, an indigenous Mongolian deity converted to the Dharma by the third Dalai Lama. He is red in colour, brandishing a sword and a trident with a fluttering banner, and wears a coat of mail. In fact his name comes from the Mongolian *begder* meaning coat of mail.

74 Full prostrations involve prostrating full-length on the ground, then raising your joined hands above your head in a gesture of salutation.

75 There is no particular need to stop at 100,000; some Tibetans accumulate millions of prostrations in the course of their lifetime. It is also possible to perform the Foundation Yogas as part of a daily practice without any concern to reaching a set number. According to Namkhai Norbu Rimpoche, this is the approach taken by Dzogchen. See *The Crystal and the Way of Light* (Note 62), p.117.

Illustration Credits

Colour plates

PLATE ONE Cakrasaṃvara thangka by permission of Dhammachari Maitreya.

PLATE TWO Vajrabhairava thangka by permission of Clear Vision.

PLATE THREE Kālacakra thangka by permission of Dhammachari Maitreya.

PLATE FOUR Vajravārāhī thangka by permission of Dhammachari Ratnachuda.

PLATE FIVE Sarvabuddhaḍākinī thangka by permission of Urgyen Sangharakshita.

PLATE SIX Mahākāla thangka by permission of Dhammachari Maitreya.

PLATE SEVEN Śrīdevī thangka by permission of Dhammachari Maitreya.

PLATE EIGHT Refuge assembly thangka by permission of Clear Vision.

Black and White Illustrations

PAGE 14 Śrī Mahā Heruka thangka by permission of Dhammachari Maitreya.

PAGE 18 Detail of Prajñāpāramitā thangka wall painting from Thöling. Photograph copyright Brian Beresford.

PAGE 30 Vajrasattva drawing by Dhammachari Aloka.

PAGE 34 Detail of Vajrasattva thangka by permission of Dhammachari Sanghaloka.

PAGE 46 Padmasambhava thangka painted by Dhammachari Chintamani.

PAGE 52 Detail of Padmasambhava thangka by permission of Dhammachari Maitreya.

PAGE 62 Milarepa detail from thangka by permission of Dhammachari Maitreya.

PAGE 70 Vajrabhairava thangka by permission of Dhammachari Danavira.

PAGE 92 Chöd ḍākinī drawing by Dhammachari Aloka.

PAGE 100 Detail of Machik Labdron thangka by permission of Dhammachari Maitreya.

PAGE 102 Siṃhamukha drawing by Dhammachari Aloka.

PAGE 110 Four Great Kings – Detail of thangka by permission of Dhammachari Maitreya.

PAGE 118 Detail of Mahākāla thangka by permission of Dhammachari Maitreya.

PAGE 120 Śrīdevī detail from Amitāyus thangka by permission of Urgyen Sangharakshita.

PAGE 132 Refuge assembly drawing by Dhammachari Aloka.

PAGE 136 Samantabhadra and Samantabhadri thangka by permission of the Rupa Company.

PAGE 138 Detail of Vajradhara thangka by permission of Dhammachari Maitreya.

Glossary

ABHIDHARMA One of the three main branches of Buddhist literature, dealing with the analysis of phenomena and mental states.

ANIMAL REALM The realm of existence in which consciousness is dominated by the struggle for survival and the basic drives for food, sex, and sleep. It may refer to actual animals or to human beings in such states of consciousness.

ARCHETYPAL REALM The objective pole of a supernormal level of consciousness. A level of heightened experience on which everything is imbued with rich symbolic meaning.

ARCHETYPE A deep patterning of the mind, which often expresses itself through myth and symbol. Archetypal experience is often tinged with a feeling of supra-personal reality.

ARHAT Originally a term of respect for someone who had gained Enlightenment. In Mahāyāna and Vajrayāna Buddhism it came to represent someone who settled for the lesser ideal of personal emancipation from suffering, in contrast to the Bodhisattva (q.v.).

ASURA Similar to the Titans of Greek mythology, asuras are powerful and jealous beings who are prepared to use force and manipulation to gain their own ends. In the Wheel of Life (q.v.) they are represented as warring with the gods. They may be seen as objectively-existent beings or as symbols for states of mind sometimes experienced by human beings. Female asuras are called asurīs and are represented as voluptuous. Asurīs play on their seductive charms to gain their own ends.

BARDO (*Tibetan*) The 'state between' two other states of being. In particular the intermediate state between one life and the next.

BHIKSHU A Buddhist mendicant (Sanskrit *bhikṣu*).

BODHICITTA The compassionate 'desire' (based not on egoistic volitions but on insight into the true nature of things) to gain Enlightenment for the benefit of all living beings. More technically, it can be divided into absolute Bodhicitta, which is synonymous with transcendental wisdom, and relative Bodhicitta – the heartfelt compassion that is the natural consequence of an experience of absolute Bodhicitta.

BODHISATTVA A being pledged to become a Buddha so as to be in the best position to help all other beings to escape from suffering by gaining Enlightenment.

BUDDHA A title, meaning one who is awake. A Buddha is someone who has gained Enlightenment – the perfection of wisdom and compassion. In particular, the title applied to Siddhārtha Gautama, also known as Śākyamuni, the founder of Buddhism.

BUDDHA FAMILY The five main groupings into which every aspect of existence – both mundane and transcendental – is divided in Tantric Buddhism. The blueprint for these groupings is provided by the mandala of the five Jinas (q.v.).

BUDDHAS, FIVE Another name for the five Jinas (q.v.).

CHAKRA Literally 'wheel'. (Anglicized, from the Sanskrit *cakra*.) Centres of energy visualized within the body in some forms of Buddhist Tantric meditation.

CLEAR LIGHT The experience of the natural state of the mind, of consciousness 'undiluted' by any tendency to move towards sensory experience. Recognition of the nature of this state is synonymous with Enlightenment.

COMPLETION STAGE The second of the two stages of Highest Tantra (q.v.). It focuses on advanced practices designed to concentrate and channel the most subtle energies of the psychophysical organism, in order to bring about the speedy attainment of Enlightenment.

CONDITIONED EXISTENCE See saṃsāra.

ḌĀKA The male equivalent of a ḍākinī.

ḌĀKINĪ A class of beings who appear in the form of women (though they may sometimes be represented with the heads of animals). They may be more or less evolved, from fiends and witches to Enlightened beings. In the Buddhist Tantra they often function as messengers, and frequently represent upsurging inspiration or non-conceptual understanding.

DAMARU A drum, usually double-headed and made either of skulls or of wood, used in some forms of Tantric meditation and ritual.

DEVA A long-lived being who experiences refined and blissful states of mind. Devas thus inhabit a heavenly realm. These realms can be interpreted as objective or as symbols for states of mind in which human beings can dwell.

DHARMA A word with numerous meanings. Among other things it can mean truth or reality. It also stands for all those teachings and methods which are conducive to gaining Enlightenment, and thereby seeing things as they truly are, particularly the teachings of the Buddha.

DHARMAKĀYA Literally 'body of truth'. The mind of a Buddha. The Enlightened experience, unmediated by concepts or symbols.

DHARMAPĀLA A protector of the Dharma. Buddhism recognizes many Dharmapālas. Some may be expressions of the Enlightened mind, others are beings on a mundane level who are sympathetic to the Dharma.

DHYĀNA A state of supernormal concentration on a wholesome object. It may occur spontaneously, but is generally the fruit of successful meditation practice. Buddhist tradition recognizes different levels of dhyāna, each one increasingly refined and satisfying.

DZOGCHEN (*Tibetan*) A set of advanced teachings and practices particularly associated with the Nyingma school (q.v.) of Tibetan Buddhism.

EMPTINESS See śūnyatā.

ENLIGHTENMENT A state of perfect wisdom and limitless compassion. The only permanently satisfying solution to the human predicament. The achievement of a Buddha.

ESOTERIC REFUGES Those Refuges (q.v.) which are matters of direct personal experience, embodied in the guru, yidam, and ḍākinī (all q.v.) by the Buddhist Tantra.

EXOTERIC REFUGES The Buddha, Dharma, and Sangha (all q.v.).

FOUNDATION YOGAS A set of meditational or yogic practices whose performance helps overcome mental hindrances and accumulate positive impressions in the mind. They can be practised in preparation for the meditations of Highest Tantra (q.v.), or purely for their own intrinsic value.

GARUḌA A species of mythical bird, enemy of the nāgas (q.v.).

GELUK By far the largest of the four main schools of Tibetan Buddhism, founded in the fourteenth century by Tsongkhapa. It emphasizes ethical discipline and training in clear thinking as a basis for meditation.

GENERATION STAGE The first of the two stages of Highest Tantra (q.v.). It focuses on the development of the vivid visualization and experience of oneself as a deity.

GESHE (*Tibetan*) A title awarded in the Kadam and Geluk schools of Tibetan Buddhism to those who have become deeply accomplished in Buddhist studies. The word *geshe* relates to the Sanskrit *kalyāṇa mitra*, meaning spiritual friend – so a *geshe* in the true sense is one who can act as a wise and learned spiritual advisor.

GOING FOR REFUGE The act of committing oneself to the attainment of Enlightenment by reliance on the three Refuges (q.v). Also refers to the ceremony by which one formally becomes a Buddhist.

GREAT BLISS A state of ecstatic happiness achieved through the realization of the illusory nature of the ego. In Highest Tantra (q.v.) it is cultivated as an integral part of contemplation of śūnyatā (q.v.).

GURU A person who through teaching and/or personal example helps other people to follow the path to Enlightenment.

HELL REALM A state of extreme physical or mental suffering, the hell realms may be understood as objective states into which one can be reborn, or as symbols for states of extreme distress experienced in the course of human life. Buddhism has no concept of a permanent state of perdition.

HERUKA A general appellation for a wrathful male Tantric deity. Also an epithet of the yidam (q.v.) Cakrasaṃvara.

HIGHEST TANTRA The most advanced of the four levels of Buddhist Tantra. It consists of the Generation and Completion stages (both q.v.).

HĪNAYĀNA The 'lesser way' or 'lesser vehicle'. Buddhist schools who do not advocate the Bodhisattva ideal. Though in common use among Mahāyāna and Vajrayāna Buddhists, the term is regarded as pejorative by the Theravāda school (q.v.).

HUMAN REALM The state of being 'truly human' – characterized by a balanced awareness of both the pleasant and painful aspects of life, and a capacity to co-operate and empathize with others. In Buddhism this state is regarded as the best starting-point from which to enter the path to Enlightenment.

HUNGRY GHOST A class of being (*preta* in Sanskrit) too overcome by craving to gain satisfaction from any experience. The idea can be interpreted literally, or symbolically as a state of mind sometimes experienced by human beings. Pretas are represented in Buddhist art with large stomachs and pinhole mouths.

JEWELS, THREE The Buddha, Dharma, and Sangha (all q.v.). The three highest values in Buddhism.

JINAS, FIVE A very important set of five Buddhas, often represented as interrelated in a mandala (q.v.) pattern. They each embody a particular Wisdom (Sanskrit *jñāna*) – an aspect of the Enlightened vision. Jina literally means 'conqueror'.

KADAM A school of Tibetan Buddhism springing from the Indian teacher Atīśa in the eleventh century. It no longer survives, but its teachings were taken over by the Gelukpas, who are sometimes referred to as the New Kadam school.

KAGYU One of the four main schools of Tibetan Buddhism, founded in the eleventh century by Gampopa. It emphasizes meditation and has produced many successful solitary meditators.

KARMA Literally 'action'. Simply stated, the so-called 'law of karma' says that our willed actions (mental and vocal as well as physical) will have consequences for us in the future. 'Skilful' actions arising from states of love, tranquillity, and wisdom, will result in happiness. 'Unskilful' actions, based on craving, aversion, and ignorance, will produce painful results.

KHAṬVĀṄGA A magic staff, usually adorned with skulls and other symbols. It is an important symbol in Tantric Buddhism.

LAMA (*Tibetan*) see guru.

LAM DRE (*Tibetan*) 'Path and Fruit', a system of teaching of the complete path to Enlightenment preserved and transmitted especially within the Sakya school (q.v.) of Tibetan Buddhism.

LAM RIM (*Tibetan*) 'Graduated Path'. A system of teaching founded by the Indian master Atīśa in which all the stages of the path to Enlightenment are laid out in a very clear and systematic manner. Each of the four main schools of Tibetan Buddhism has produced Lam Rim texts.

LOWER TANTRAS The first three of the four main divisions of Buddhist Tantra (q.v.): action (Sanskrit *kriyā*), performance (Sanskrit *caryā*), and union (Sanskrit *yoga*).

MADHYAMAKA A school of Mahāyāna thought founded by the Indian teacher Nāgārjuna. It is characterized by a denial that concepts can ever accurately describe Reality.

MAHĀSIDDHAS, EIGHTY-FOUR An important set of Enlightened Tantric practitioners.

MAHĀYĀNA The 'great way' or 'great vehicle'. Those schools of Buddhism that teach the Bodhisattva ideal – of selfless striving to gain Enlightenment so as to be in the best possible position to help all other living beings to escape from suffering.

MAHĀYĀNA PATHS, FIVE Five stages of the path to Enlightenment, according to the Mahāyāna. They are the stages of accumulation, preparation, seeing, meditation, and 'no more learning'.

MANDALA A word with various meanings in different contexts. In this book it means a pattern of elements around a central focus. Ideal mandalas are often used as objects of meditation in Buddhist Tantra.

MANTRA A string of sound-symbols recited to concentrate and protect the mind. Many Buddhist figures have mantras associated with them. Through reciting their mantra one deepens one's connection with the aspect of Enlightenment which the figure embodies.

MĀRA The Buddhist personification of everything that tends to promote suffering and hinder growth towards Enlightenment. It literally means 'death'.

MERITS The positive states generated through the performance of virtuous actions, which predispose one to encounter happy and fortunate circumstances.

MUDRĀ Can be the general term for a Tantric emblem. In this book it is used in its sense of a hand gesture imbued with symbolic significance. In Tantric Buddhism it can also refer to a female consort.

NĀGA A class of powerful serpents associated with water. They have something of the same symbolism as dragons, being guardians of treasures, and associated with wisdom.

NIRVĀṆA The state of Enlightenment, the cessation of suffering. For the Mahāyāna (q.v.) it became a lesser ideal – a state of blissful happiness in which one could settle down rather than working compassionately to help all other beings to attain the same happy state.

NYINGMA The oldest of the four main schools of Tibetan Buddhism, deriving its original inspiration from the Indian teacher Padmasambhava, who went to Tibet in the eighth century.

PANDIT An Indian scholar.

PERFECTION (Sanskrit *pāramitā*) The main positive qualities that the Bodhisattva (q.v.) strives to develop. A positive quality only becomes a *pāramitā* in the full sense when it is imbued with transcendental wisdom. The six perfections constitute the most important list of positive qualities in Mahāyāna (q.v.) Buddhism: generosity, ethics, patience, effort, meditation, and wisdom.

POISONS, FIVE Ignorance, hatred, pride, craving, and envy. Known as *kleśas* in Sanskrit.

PRAJÑĀ Direct intuitive apprehension of the real nature of things. This is usually brought about by (1) listening to the Buddhist teachings, (2) reflecting upon them, (3) meditating upon them.

PURE LAND A realm created through the meditative concentration and meritorious actions of a Buddha, in which beings can be reborn. In a Pure Land, conditions are totally favourable for progress towards Buddhahood. Also, the schools of Buddhism whose practice centres on being reborn in such realms.

REALMS, SIX A classification of all the possibilities for rebirth within conditioned existence. They are the realms of the devas, asuras, humans, animals, hungry ghosts, and beings in hell (all q.v.). The six realms are pictorially represented in the Wheel of Life (q.v.).

REFLEX Certain of the five Jinas can appear in a second form, which demonstrates another aspect of their Wisdom. This second form is sometimes described as the 'reflex' of the Jina.

REFUGE One of the things on which Buddhism believes it is wise to rely. The three Refuges – the Buddha, the Dharma, and the Sangha – are common to all forms of Buddhism. The Esoteric Refuges (q.v.) are peculiar to Buddhist Tantra.

RIMPOCHE (OR RINPOCHE) (*Tibetan*) An honorific title for a Tibetan Buddhist master – especially one who is believed to be the rebirth or emanation of a previous highly-developed Buddhist practitioner. It literally means 'precious one'.

SĀDHANA A general Sanskrit word for one's personal religious practice. More specifically, a Buddhist Tantric practice usually involving visualization and mantra recitation. The written text of such a Tantric practice.

SAKYA One of the four main schools of Tibetan Buddhism, deriving its original inspiration from the Indian Tantric master Virūpa.

SAMAYA The commitments one takes upon oneself on receiving Vajrayāna (q.v.) initiation.

SAṀSĀRA The cyclic round of birth and death, marked by suffering and frustration, which can only be brought to an end by the attainment of Enlightenment.

SANGHA In the widest sense, the community of all those who are following the path to Buddhahood. As one of the Refuges (q.v.) it refers to the Ārya or Noble Sangha – those Buddhist practitioners who have gained insight into the true nature of things and whose progress towards Buddhahood is certain. In other contexts the term can refer to those who have taken ordination as Buddhist monks or nuns.

SEED SYLLABLE Subtle sound-symbols through which Enlightened beings can communicate the Dharma to those on advanced stages of the path to Enlightenment. They are often visualized in Tantric meditation.

ŚĀKYAMUNI The 'sage of the Śākyans', an epithet of Siddhārtha Gautama, the founder of Buddhism.

SIDDHI Supernormal attainments (such as telepathy) gained through meditation, especially using the methods of Buddhist Tantra. Enlightenment is the supreme *siddhi*.

SKILFUL MEANS See upāya.

SPIRITUAL In this book, spiritual means concerned with the development of higher states of consciousness, especially with the path to Enlightenment. In this context it has nothing to do with spirits or spiritualism.

STUPA Originally a mound or structure built to commemorate a Buddha or other highly-developed person, and often containing relics. It became a symbol for the mind of a Buddha.

SUBTLE BODY A subtle counterpart to the physical body, made up of refined psychophysical energies, which is visualized in some forms of Tantric meditation.

ŚŪNYATĀ Literally 'emptiness' or 'voidness'. The ultimate nature of existence, the absolute aspect of all cognizable things. The doctrine of śūnyatā holds that all phenomena are empty (*śūnya*) of any permanent unchanging self or essence. By extension, it can mean the transcendental (q.v.) experience brought about by direct intuitive insight into the empty nature of things.

SŪTRA Literally 'thread'. A discourse given by the Buddha, or by one of his senior disciples and approved by him, and included in the Buddhist canon. *Sūtra* is Sanskrit; the Pali is *sutta*.

TANTRA A form of Buddhism making use of yogic practices of visualization, mantra, mudrā, and mandalas (all q.v.), as well as symbolic ritual, and meditations which work with subtle psychophysical energies. Also (lower case) the Buddhist texts, often couched in symbolic language, in which these practices are described.

TATHĀGATA A title of the Buddha. Can mean 'one thus gone' or 'one thus come'. A Buddha goes from the world through wisdom – seeing its illusory nature. He comes into it through compassion – in order to teach living beings how to put an end to suffering.

THANGKA (*Tibetan*) A Tibetan religious painting.

THERAVĀDA The 'School of the Elders' – the form of Buddhism prevalent in Thailand, Burma, and Sri Lanka.

TITAN See asura.

TRANSCENDENTAL (Sanskrit *lokottara*). Experience that goes beyond the cyclic, mundane round of birth and death. The experience or viewpoint of an Enlightened being.

TRUTHS, TWO The ultimate truth (Sanskrit *paramārtha satya*) and the relative truth (Sanskrit *saṃvṛti satya*). According to the Mahāyāna view, the ultimate truth is the true nature of Reality, śūnyatā, the absence of inherent existence of all phenomena; this can never be adequately described in words. The relative truth is the conceptual formulations of Reality taught by the Buddha, such as the law of conditionality (Sanskrit *pratītya samutpāda*).

UPĀYA The skilful methods compassionately employed by Buddhas and others to interest people in the Dharma and encourage them to follow the path to Enlightenment.

VAJRA A ritual sceptre, which symbolically combines the qualities of both diamond and thunderbolt.

VAJRAGURU A master and teacher of Buddhist Tantra.

VAJRAYĀNA The 'way of the diamond thunderbolt' – Buddhist Tantra (q.v.) of India and the Himalayan region.

VISUALIZATION A common method of Buddhist meditation, involving the use of imagination to create vivid symbolic forms.

WHEEL OF LIFE A graphic representation in one painting of the whole process through which craving, hatred, and ignorance cause living beings to circle in states of unsatisfactoriness. It includes depictions of the six realms of devas, asuras, humans, animals, hungry ghosts, and beings in hell (all q.v.), which together represent all the mental states unenlightened living beings can experience.

WISDOMS, FIVE The Wisdoms of the five Jinas (q.v.): the Mirror-Like Wisdom, Wisdom of Equality, Discriminating Wisdom, All-Accomplishing Wisdom, and the Wisdom of the Dharmadhātu (sphere of reality).

YAB-YUM (*Tibetan*) Literally an honorific term for 'father-mother'. The Tibetan term for a Buddha or other deity represented in sexual union with a consort.

YĀNA A 'way' or 'vehicle' which can be used for attaining Buddhahood. One of the great streams of thought and teaching (embracing a number of schools) that have appeared in the development of Buddhism. (*See* Hīnayāna, Mahāyāna, Vajrayāna).

YIDAM (*Tibetan*) A Buddhist meditational deity embodying an aspect of Enlightenment. The term is sometimes reserved for meditational deities visualized in Highest Tantra (q.v.).

YOGA A Sanskrit word meaning union. In Buddhist Tantra it refers to a method of meditation or physical exercise designed to bring about spiritual development.

YOGIN A male practitioner of yoga. The term is applied particularly to adepts of Buddhist Tantra.

YOGINĪ A female practitioner of yoga; a female Tantric adept.

ZEN (*Japanese*) A school of Mahāyāna Buddhism found mainly in Japan and Korea. 'Zen' is derived from the Sanskrit word *dhyāna* meaning meditation, and Zen places great emphasis on the practice of seated meditation. It aims not to rely on words and logical concepts for communicating the Dharma, often preferring to employ action or paradoxes.

Selected Reading

General

David L. Snellgrove, *Indo-Tibetan Buddhism*, Serindia, 1987.
Blanche Christine Olschak and Geshe Thupten Wangyal, *Mystic Art of Ancient Tibet*, Shambhala, 1987.
Marilyn M. Rhie and Robert A.E. Thurman, *The Sacred Art of Tibet*, Thames and Hudson, 1991.

Chapter One

Lama Thubten Yeshe, *Introduction to Tantra*, Wisdom Publications, 1987.
John Blofeld, *The Way of Power*, George Allen and Unwin, 1970.
Herbert V. Guenther and Chögyam Trungpa, *The Dawn of Tantra*, Shambhala, 1975.
H.H. the Dalai Lama, Tsongkhapa, and Jeffrey Hopkins, *Deity Yoga*, Snow Lion, 1981.
H.H. the Dalai Lama, Tsongkhapa, and Jeffrey Hopkins, *Tantra in Tibet*, Snow Lion, 1987.
Sangharakshita, *Creative Symbols of Tantric Buddhism*, Windhorse Publications, 2002.

Chapter Two

The Perfection of Wisdom in 8,000 Lines and its Verse Summary, trans. Edward Conze, Four Seasons Foundation, 1973.
Buddhist Wisdom Books, trans. Edward Conze, Unwin, 1988.
Geshe Kelsang Gyatso, *Heart of Wisdom*, Tharpa, 1986.

Chapter Three

Mahāyāna Purification, ed. and trans. Brian Beresford, Library of Tibetan Works and Archives, 1980.
Jamgon Kongtrul, *The Torch of Certainty*, Shambhala, 1977.

Geshe Rabten, *Preliminary Practices of Tibetan Buddhism*, Wisdom Publications, 1982.
Khetsun Sangpo Rinbochay, *Tantric Practice in Nyingma*, ed. and trans. Jeffrey Hopkins, Rider, 1982.

Chapter Four

Buddha's Lions, trans. James B. Robinson, Dharma Publishing, 1979.
Keith Dowman, *Masters of Mahāmudrā*, State University of New York Press, 1985.
The XIIth Khentin Tai Situpa, *Tilopa (Some Glimpses of his Life)*, ed. and trans. Kenneth Holmes, Dzalendara, 1988.
Herbert V. Guenther, *The Life and Teaching of Nāropa*, Oxford University Press, 1963.
The Life of Marpa the Translator, trans. Nalanda Translation Committee directed by Chögyam Trungpa, Prajna Press, 1982.
The Hundred Thousand Songs of Milarepa (2 volumes), trans. Garma C. C. Chang, Shambhala, 1977.
The Life of Milarepa, trans. Lobsang P. Lhalungpa, Shambhala, 1984.
Chogay Trichen, *The History of the Sakya Tradition*, Ganesha, 1983.
Peter Meyer, *H.H. Sakya Trizin and the Sakyapa Tradition*, Orgyen Cho Ling, 1978.
The Life and Teachings of Tsongkhapa, ed. and trans. Robert Thurman, Library of Tibetan Works and Archives, 1982.
Geshe Wangyal, *The Door of Liberation*, Wisdom Publications, 1995.
Selected Works of the Dalai Lama, trans. Glenn Mullin, Snow Lion. A series of translations. To date includes volumes on the first, second, third, seventh and thirteenth Dalai Lamas.
Dudjom Rimpoche, *The Nyingma School of Tibetan Buddhism, Its Fundamentals and History* (2 vols), Wisdom Publications, 1991.
Yeshe Tsogyal, *The Life and Liberation of Padmasambhava* (2 vols), Dharma Publishing, 1978.

Chapter Five

The Dalai Lama and Jeffrey Hopkins, *Kalachakra Tantra, Rite of Initiation*, Wisdom Publications, 1988.
Daniel Cozort, *Highest Yoga Tantra*, Snow Lion, 1986.
F.D. Lessing and A. Wayman, *Introduction to the Buddhist Tantric Systems*, Motilal Banarsidass, 1978.

Chapter Six

Geshe Kelsang Gyatso, *A Guide to Dakiniland*, Tharpa, 1991.
Lama Yeshe, *Vajra Yogini*, Wisdom Publications, 1984.
Tsultrim Allione, *Women of Wisdom*, Arkana, 1986.

Nam-mkha'i snying-po, *Mother of Knowledge: The Enlightenment of Yeshe Tsogyal*, trans. Tarthang Tulku, Dharma Publishing, 1983.

Chapter Seven

Rene de Nebesky-Wojkowitz, *Oracles and Demons of Tibet*, Mouton, 1956.
Lama Lodro, *The Invocation of Mahakala*, Kagyu Droden Kunchab, 1985.

Index

A
Abhidharma 159
adi-Buddha 31, 86
Ākāśadhāteśvarī 12
Akṣobhya 7, 11, 31, 84
  and Vajrasattva 42
Akṣobhyavajra 86
Amitābha 7, 11, 50, 141
Amoghasiddhi 7, 12, 59
Amṛtakuṇḍalin 128
anger 87, *see also* hatred
animal realm 159
anuttarayoga 4, 16, 32, 71, 162
archetype 159
archetypal realm 159
ardha pariyaṅka 84
arhat 137, 159
art 148
Ārya school 86
Aṣṭasāhasrikā 22
asura 159
Athena 25, 29
Atīśa 66, 89
attachment 75
avadhūtī 9, 126
Avalokiteśvara 113

B
Baiṣajyaguru 141
bardo 13, 159
Bardo Thödol, see Tibetan Book of the Dead
beauty 29
begging-bowl 26
Bektse 155
bell 15, 33
Bhairava 75
bhikshu 51, 159
bindu 9
Birwapa 64
black magic 123, 154
Black Master of Life 81
Black-Cloaked Lord 119
bodhicitta 160
bodhisattva 135, 160
Bonpo 49
bow and arrow 97, 101
Brahmā 122
Buddha 160
  consort 11, *see also yab-yum*
  five 35
  Medicine 141
  wrathful *see* heruka
  see also Śākyamuni
Buddha Field *see* Pure Land

Buddhahood 27,
see also Enlightenment, nirvāṇa
Buddha-nature 151
Buddha Refuge, esoteric 48
Buddha śramaṇa mudrā 141

C

Cakrasaṃvara 64, 74, 77, 139, 140, 153
Caṇḍālī 85, 121
caryā tantra 4
chakra 160
Chöd Rite 98, 101
Chogyal Phakpa 65
Cilupā 89
Clear Light 160
communication 108
Completion Stage 160
conditioned co-production 78
confession 39
consort 11, *see also yab-yum*
Conze, E. 24
Copper-Coloured Mountain 151
craving 10, *see also* desire, greed

D

ḍāka 93, 142, 154, 160
ḍākinī 50, 79, 93ff, 108, 137, 142, 154, 160
orders of 97
Refuge 108
Dakmema 61, 84
Dakpo Lharje 63
Dalai Lama 68, 88, 123
damaru 53, 160
death 10, 12, 36, 41
desire 77, *see also* craving, greed
deva 161
devotion 144
Dharma 161
Dharma Refuge, esoteric 73
Dharmadhātu, Wisdom of the 12
dharmakāya 98, 161
Dharmakīrti 65
dharmapāla 113ff, 128, 137, 142, 161
Dharmatāla 142
dhīḥ 26
Dhṛtarāṣṭra 129
dhyāna 11, 161
Diamond Sūtra 22
Dīpaṇkara 135
Dōgen 147
Ḍombinī 121
dorje *see* vajra
Dorje Chang 53
Dorje Drolo 54
Dorje Jikje 80
Dorje Lekpa 127
Dorje Naljorma 95
Dorje Phamo 99
Dorlek 127
Drakpa Gyaltsen 65
Drokmi 64
Drukpa Kagyu 124
Du Kyi Khorlo 88
duality 15
Dukhor 88
Dunsum Khyenpa 63
dvarapāla 128
Dzogchen 126, 139, 161

E

earth-touching mudrā 140
ego 44, 115
eight pure disciples 67
eighteen arhats 142
Ekajaṭā 126, 139
Ekamātri Śrīdevī 121
Ekavīra 82
empowerment *see* initiation
emptiness *see* śūnyatā
energy, and Tantra 8
Enlightenment 161,
see also Buddhahood, nirvāṇa

Esoteric Refuges 48, 73, 93, 107, 161
Exoteric Refuges 108, 137, 161

F

family, Buddha 160
  Vajra 81
Father Tantra 72, 78, 87
Field of Merit 133
Foundation Yoga 33, 144, 150, 161
Four-Faced Lord 119
Four Great Kings 129, 142
friendship 47, 108

G

Gampopa 63
Ganden Tripa 67
Gandenpa 67
gandharva 129
Ganesha 119
Garab Dorje 139
Garpa Nakpo 128
garuḍa 13, 161
Gedundrup 68
Geluk school 66, 67, 74, 87, 140, 161
generation stage 162
geshe 162
Godan Khan 65
Going for Refuge 51, 142, 162, *see also* prostration, refuge
Gonpo Nakpo Chenpo 113
Great Bliss 162
greed 75, *see also* craving, desire
Green Tārā 12, 127
guardian *see* dharmapāla, lokapāla
Guhyasamāja 85, 140
  Tantra 85
guilt 36
guru 4, 47, 51, 117, 137, 151, 162
Guru Rimpoche *see* Padmasambhava
Guru Yoga 49, 98
Gyaltshap Je 67
Gyepa Dorje 83
gyulu 81
Gyume 87
Gyuto 87

H

Hakuin 147
hatred 7, 10, *see also* anger
Hayagrīva 54, 115, 128
Heart Sūtra 22, 24, 26, 28
hell realm 36, 162
heruka 13, 74, 81, 162
Heruka Cakrasaṃvara 74
Hevajra 64, 83, 140
Hevajra Tantra 83
Hīnayāna 162
horse 129
Hui Neng 82, 147
hūṃ 35
human realm 162
hungry ghosts 162
Hva-shang 142

I

imagination 3, 20
impermanence 12, *see also* death
Indrabhūti 83, 85, 153
initiation 72, 88
  Tantric 48, 56
insubstantiality 103
intellect 25

J

Jewel Ornament of Liberation 63
Jewels, Three 163, *see also* refuge
Jinas, five 163
Jñānapada school 86
Jung, C.G. 29, 142, 145

K

Kadam 66, 163
Kagyu lineage 59ff
Kagyu school 74, 84, 99, 139, 163

Kālacakra 88, 140
Kālacakra mandala 88
Kālarātri 75, 77
kalyāṇa mitra 47, 108
Kāmadeva 89, 101
Kanakamuni 141
Kapāladhara Hevajra 84
karma 33, 36, 163
Karma Kagyu 63
Kāśyapa 141
khandroma 93
khaṭvāṅga 57, 76, 163
Khedrup Je 67
Khon Khonchok Gyalpo 64
Khorlo Demchok 74
Khorlo Dompa 74
Khyungpo Naljor 94
king of Zahor 55, 135
kleśas 165
Krakucchanda 141
kriyā tantra 4
Krodheśvarī 13
Kublai Khan 65
Kukkurīpa 94
Kulika 89
Kunga Nyingpo 64
Kuntuzangpo 139
Kurukullā 101, 154
Kyedorje 83
Kyungpo Naljor 95

L

Lam Dre 64, 163
Lam Rim 67, 163
Lam Rim Chenmo 67
lineage 49
lion 68
literature 19
Locanā 11
Lodan Choksey 54
lokapāla 85, 129, 142
Lord of the Tent 119
lotus 24
Lotus family 128
Lower Tantras 163
Lozang Drakpa 66

M

ma za dam sum 125
Ma Zhang 49
Machik Labdron 101
Machik Paldan Lhamo 122
Madhyamaka 163
magic 4, 58, 154
  and Tantra 7
  hermetic 15
mahā 8
Mahākāla 113, 119, 142
mahākālī 124
mahāsiddha 8, 59, 163
mahāsukha 54
Mahāyāna 164
  sūtras 2
Maitreya 135, 140
Maitrīpada 79
mālā 25
Māmakī 11
mandala 164
  of five Buddhas 86
  of Hevajra 85
  of Kālacakra 88
Mañjuśrī 25, 65, 67, 80, 140, *see also* Yamāntaka
Mañjuśrīkīrti 89
Mañjuvajra 86, 153
mantra 164
  Padmasambhava 55
  Prajñāpāramitā 28
  Tsongkhapa 69
  Vajrasattva 35, 38
Manuṣi Buddha 140
Māra 26, 84, 164
Mārīcī 127
Marpa 20, 61, 84, 149

māyā 82ff
māyākāya 81
Medicine Buddha 141
meditation
on śūnyatā 9
see also dhyāna, visualization
Menlha 141
Menlha Deshek gye 141
merit 164
Mikmizang 129
Milarepa 61, 84
Mongolia 65
mongoose 129
moon 76
Mother Tantras 72, 75
mudrā 164
Buddha śramaṇa 141
earth touching 140
tarjanī 79
of turning… 68, 141
of Vajradhara 59
vajrahuṃkāra 76
vārada 141
vitarka 141
mūla yoga 251

N
nadi 9
nāga 22, 153, 164
Nāgārjuna 22, 85
Nairātmyā 64, 84, 153
Nālandā 64
Namthore 129
Naro Khacho 99
Nāropa 60, 89, 95
nectar 57
Niguma 94, 101
nirvāṇa 15, 164, *see also*
Enlightenment, Buddhahood
non-duality 103
non-dual tantras 153
Nyima Odzer 54
Nyingma Refuge Tree 135
Nyingma school 49, 124, 164

P
Padmasambhava 49ff, 94, 103, 124,
135
mantra 55
Paldan Lhamo 121
Paldan Makzor Gyalmo 123
Pali suttas 2
Pāṇḍaravāsinī 11
pandit 164
Pandita 89
pāramitā 164
Pema Gyalpo 53
perfection 164
Perfection of Wisdom 20ff, 67
Phabongka Rimpoche 67
Phadampa Sangye 101
Phak Kye po 129
Phakpa 89
phurba 53
pig 99
poetry 19
poisons, five 165
prajñā 11, 77, 165
Prajñāpāramitā 20ff
Prajñāpāramitā Hṛdaya see Heart Sūtra
prāṇa 9
pratītya samutpāda 78
preta 162
pride 144
prostration 32, 143, 155
Pure Land 165
purification 33
purity 31ff, 37, 40

Q
Quicksilver 81

R

Rāhu 125
Rāhula 125, 139
Rākṣasi 121
Ralchikma 126
Ratnaguṇasaṃcayagāthā 22
Ratnasambhava 7, 11
Reality 42
realms, six 165
rebirth 41
reflex 165
refuge
  esoteric 48, 73, 93, 107, 161, 165
  exoteric 108, 137, 161, 165
Refuge Tree 133ff
return journey, myth of 37
Rikjema 101
Ri-me 147
rimpoche 165
Rinchen Zangpo 85
royal ease 53
Rudra 89, 115, 128

S

Sachen Kunga Nyingpo 64
Saddharma Puṇḍarīka 37
sādhana 165
Sādhanamālā 26
Sakya Pandita 65, 89
Sakya school 64, 83, 99, 165
Śākyamuni 21, 53, 140, 141, 147, 160, 166
Śākya Senge 53
Samantabhadra 139
Samantabhadri 139
samaya 38, 40, 47, 165
Śambara 74
saṃgrahakāya 134
saṃsāra 15, 165
Saṃvara 74
Samye 50
Sangdu 85
sangha 165
Sangha Refuge, esoteric 93, 107
Sangharakshita 147
Sangwa Sherap 123
Sangwadupa 85
Sangye Rapdun 140
Śāntarakṣita 49
Saraha 74, 85
Sarvabuddhaḍākinī 99
Śastradhara Hevajra 84
Śavaripā 101
seed syllable 26, 35, 124, 166
Senge Dongchenma 103
Senge Dradok 54
sex 10ff
  Tantric *see yab-yum*
Shambhala 89
Sherapkyi Pharoltuchinma 23
Shinjeshe 80
Shiva 73, 75
siddha 8, 49
siddhi 8, 166
Śikhin 141
Siṃhalī 121
Siṃhamukha 103, 139
Siṃhavaktrā 103
skilful means 11, 42, 55, 56, 79, 87, 121, 167
skull cup 57
Sonam Tsemo 65
Sophia 29
Sparśavajrā 86
spiritual 166
spiritual friendship 47, 108
Śrīdevī 121, 142, 155
staff 58
stupa 166
subtle body 166
Sucandra 89
sun 54, 66
śūnyatā 9, 166
sūtra 2, 4, 166

Sūtra of Golden Light 129
Sūtrayāna 2, 6, 10
sword 15, 25, 66, 69, 82, 86, 121, 129, 140

T

T'ien T'ai school 146
Tamdin 128
tanrungma 124
Tantra 4ff, 33, 42, 47, 84, 95, 115, 166
  Highest *see anuttarayoga*
  Lower 4, 72
Tārā 11, 12, 127
tarjanī mudrā 79
Tarot 29
Tathāgata 166
teacher 47, 117, *see also* guru
Tenbay Nyima 68
Tenzin Gyatso 68
terma 103
thangka 167
Theravāda 167
third eye 86
Tholing 24
Three Jewels 163, *see also* refuge
Three White Ones 66
Tibet 50
Tibetan Book of the Dead 41, 115, 128
Tilopa 59, 104
time 88
tradition 148
transcendental 167
Trisong Detsen 49
truths, two 167
Tsechikma 126
Tshokyi Dorje 53
Tsongkhapa 66, 83, 89, 140
  mantra 69
tummo 61, 83, 98
Two Red Ones 66

U

Uḍḍiyāna 50
Ugrā Tārā 127
Uma 75
Upāli-Paripṛcchā Sūtra 140
upāya see skilful means
Urgyen Dorje Chang 53

V

Vaiḍūryaprabharāja 141
Vairocana 7, 12
Vaiśravaṇa 84, 129
vajra 25, 33, 42, 43, 83, 167
Vajra family 87
vajra-bell 35
Vajrabhairava 80, 153
Vajracchedikā 22
vajra-chopper 96
Vajradhara 4, 53, 59, 69, 139, 140
vajraghaṇṭā 35
vajraguru 47, 49, 93, 167
vajrahuṃkāra mudrā 76
Vajrakīla 54
Vajrapāṇi 115, 153
Vajrasādhu 127, 139
Vajrasattva 31ff, 139
  mantra 35, 38
Vajraśṛṅkalā 153
Vajravairocanī 101
Vajravārāhī 76, 99, 139, 153
Vajravārṇanī 101
Vajrayāna 3ff, 167 *see also* Tantra
Vajrayoginī 95, 98, 140
vārada mudrā 141
Vetālī 82
Viṣukalpa 85
Vijaya 128
Vimalakīrti Nirdeśa 129
Vipaśyin 140
Virūḍhaka 129
Virūpa 64, 65
Virūpākṣa 129

visualization 167
Viśvabhū 141
Viśvamāṭa 90
vitarka mudrā 141
vulture 58

W

weapons 12, 15
Wheel of Life 167
White Tārā 11
wisdom 25, 77
Wisdoms, five 167
wrathful figures *see* heruka

Y

yab-yum 11, 77, 79, 86, 149, 168
yakṣa 73, 129
Yama 84
Yamāntaka 80, 81, 128, 140
yāna 168
Yeshe Tsogyal 58, 103
yidam 71ff, 137, 168
yoga 168
  Foundation 32
  mūla 32
yoga tantra 4
yogin 168
yoginī 168
yuganaddha 77
Yulkhorsung 129

Z

Za 125, 126
Zen 16, 168

Windhorse Publications is a Buddhist publishing house, staffed by practising Buddhists. We place great emphasis on producing books of high quality, accessible and relevant to those interested in Buddhism at whatever level. Drawing on the whole range of the Buddhist tradition, our books include translations of traditional texts, commentaries, books that make links with Western culture and ways of life, biographies of Buddhists, and works on meditation.

As a charitable institution we welcome donations to help us continue our work. We also welcome manuscripts on aspects of Buddhism or meditation. To join our email list, leave your address on our website. For orders and catalogues log on to www.windhorsepublications.com or contact:

Windhorse Publications
38 Newmarket Road
Cambridge CB5 8DT
UK

Perseus Distribution
1094 Flex Drive
Jackson TN 38301
USA

Windhorse Books
P O Box 574
Newtown NSW 2042
Australia

Windhorse Publications is an arm of the Friends of the Western Buddhist Order, which has more than sixty centres on four continents. Through these centres, members of the Western Buddhist Order offer regular programmes of events for the general public and for more experienced students. These include meditation classes, public talks, study on Buddhist themes and texts, and bodywork classes such as t'ai chi, yoga, and massage. The FWBO also runs several retreat centres and the Karuna Trust, a fundraising charity that supports social welfare projects in the slums and villages of southern Asia.

Many FWBO centres have residential spiritual communities and ethical businesses associated with them. Arts activities are encouraged too, as is the development of strong bonds of friendship between people who share the same ideals. In this way the FWBO is developing a unique approach to Buddhism, not simply as a set of techniques, but as a creatively directed way of life for people living in the modern world.

If you would like more information about the FWBO please visit the website at www.fwbo.org or write to

London Buddhist Centre
51 Roman Road
London
E2 0HU
UK

Aryaloka
14 Heartwood Circle
Newmarket NH 03857
USA

Sydney Buddhist Centre
24 Enmore Road
Sydney NSW 2042
Australia

ALSO FROM WINDHORSE PUBLICATIONS

The Breath

by Vessantara

The breath: always with us, necessary to our very existence, but often unnoticed. Yet giving it attention can transform our lives.

This is a very useful combination of practical instruction on the mindfulness of breathing with much broader lessons on where the breath can lead us. Vessantara, a meditator of many years experience, offers us:

- ★ Clear instruction on how to meditate on the breath
- ★ Practical ways to integrate meditation into our lives
- ★ Suggestions for deepening calm and concentration
- ★ Advice on how to let go and dive into experience
- ★ Insights into the lessons of the breath

The Breath returns us again and again to the fundamental and precious experience of being alive.

144 pages
ISBN 978 1 899579 69 3
£6.99/$10.95/€10.95

An interesting in-depth investigation into the art of breathing.
Yoga magazine

The Heart

by Vessantara

The Heart offers ways to discover your emotional potential through an exploration of the practice of loving-kindness meditation.

Vessantara has practised this meditation for over thirty years. Here he shares his experience, gently encouraging us to unlock what is in our hearts and helping us to gain greater enjoyment from life. Among other benefits, using the exercises and meditations in this book you can:

- ★ Increase your emotional awareness
- ★ Feel more at ease with yourself
- ★ Become kinder and more open-hearted
- ★ Discover how to be more patient
- ★ Engage more spontaneously with life.

The Heart provides clear instruction and helpful suggestions for those new to meditation as well as more experienced practitioners.

176 pages
ISBN 9781 899579 71 6
£6.99/$10.95/€10.95

—the art of meditation series—

Buddhism: Tools for Living Your Life

by Vajragupta

This book is a guide for those seeking a meaningful spiritual path while living everyday lives full of families, work, and friends. Vajragupta provides clear explanations of Buddhist teachings and guidance applying these to enrich our busy and complex lives.

The personal stories, exercises, reflections, and questions in this book help transform Buddhist practice into more than a fine set of ideals. They make the path of ethics, meditation, and wisdom a tangible part of our lives.

> *In this book I have attempted to convey a feeling for what a 'Buddhist life' might be like – the underlying flavour, or ethos, of such a life. I hope I have made it clear that this way of life is possible for anyone – whatever their background and experience. My aim is to make the teachings as accessible and relevant as possible, and to give you some 'tools' with which to live a spiritual life.*

"I'm very pleased that someone has finally written this book! At last, a real 'toolkit' for living a Buddhist life. His practical suggestions are hard to resist!"

Saddhanandi, Chair of Taraloka,
named Retreat Centre of the Year 2006 by *The Good Retreat Guide*

192 pages
ISBN 9781 899579 74 7
£10.99/$16.95/€16.95

Creative Symbols of Tantric Buddhism

by Sangharakshita

Tantric Buddhism is concerned with the direct experience of who we are and what we can become. For the Tantra this experience cannot be meditated by concepts, but it can be evoked with the help of symbols.

This is a thorough and informative introduction to:

- The symbolism of colour, mantras, and the mandala of the five Buddhas
- The Tibetan Wheel of Life – a map of our mind and emotions
- Figures of the Tantric tradition – Buddhas, Bodhisattvas, dakinis, and the archetypal guru
- The symbolism of ritual objects and offerings
- Confronting and transforming our fear of crisis situations and death

224 pages, with b&w illustrations
ISBN 978 1 899579 47 1
£10.99/$19.95/€19.95

OTHER BOOKS IN THIS SERIES

A Guide to the Buddhas
by Vessantara

Why does Buddhism refer to so many Buddhas? Who are they and what can they tell us about ourselves? In this book we meet the historical and archetypal Buddhas who form part of the rich symbolism of Tibetan Buddhism. This is an informative guide for those new to Buddhism and a handy reference for more experienced practitioners. Vessantara, with more than thirty-five years of meditation experience, combines the power of story-telling with practical guidance and brings the Buddhas and their visualization practices to life.

176 pages, illustrated
£11.99/$18.95/€18.95
ISBN 978 1 899579 83 9

A Guide to the Bodhisattvas
by Vessantara

When we meet with one of the Bodhisattvas – whether in a painting or sculpture or visualized in meditation – we are brought face to face with a being that embodies Enlightenment. An encounter with such a figure is likely to move us far more deeply than a list of the qualities of someone who is enlightened. Bodhisattvas are dedicated to helping ordinary people on the path towards Enlightenment. This guide introduces a panoply of these figures from the vast array within the Buddhist tradition. In meeting Tārā, the rescuer, Mañjuśrī, the Bodhisattva of Wisdom, Avalokiteśvara, the Bodhisattva of Compassion, and many others, we become transformed by their qualities.

128 pages, illustrated
£11.99/$18.95/€18.95
ISBN 978 1 899579 84 6